Martin Agricola (ca. 1486–1556) was an important early Lutheran musician and teacher in Saxony and his treatises were intended as textbooks in musical performance. Highly illustrated, his books on musical instruments give practical instruction on a number of instruments of his time, showing methods of fingering, tuning and notation. As such they are valuable sources of information about the study and performance of music in Germany in the early sixteenth century. The first *Musica instrumentalis deudsch*, written mostly in rhymed German verse and containing woodcut diagrams and depictions of musical instruments, was published in Wittenberg in 1529. It was modelled on the *Musica getutscht* (Basel, 1511) of Sebastian Virdung, copying many of the woodcuts found in the earlier work and redefining its classification of musical instruments. Agricola gives fingering charts for the woodwinds, tunings and tablature for plucked and bowed strings, and descriptions of keyboards. A revised and almost completely rewritten edition of Agricola's treatise was published in 1545. Both these treatises appear here together for the first time in English translation.

The 'Musica instrumentalis deudsch'
of Martin Agricola

CAMBRIDGE MUSICAL TEXTS AND MONOGRAPHS

The series Cambridge Musical Texts and Monographs has as its centres of interest the history of performance and the history of instruments. It includes annotated translations of important historical documents, authentic historical texts on music, and monographs on various aspects of historical performance.

Published

Ian Woodfield *The Early History of the Viol*

Rebecca Harris-Warrick (trans. and ed.) *Principles of the Harpsichord by Monsieur de Saint Lambert*

Robin Stowell *Violin Technique and Performance Practice in the Late Eighteenth and Early Nineteenth Centuries*

Vincent J. Panetta (trans. and ed.) *Treatise on Harpsichord Tuning by Jean Denis*

John Butt *Bach Interpretation*

Grant O'Brien *Ruckers: A Harpsichord and Virginal Building Tradition*

Nicholas Thistlethwaite *The Making of the Victorian Organ*

Christopher Page (trans. and ed.) *Summa musicae: A Thirteenth-Century Manual for Singers*

Ardal Powell (trans. and ed.) *The Virtuoso Flute-Player by Johann Georg Tromlitz*

Keith Polk *German Instrumental Music in the Late Middle Ages*

Beth Bullard (trans. and ed.) *Musica getutscht: A Treatise on Musical Instruments (1511) by Sebastian Virdung*

David Rowland *A History of Pianoforte Pedalling*

John Butt *Music Education and the Art of Performance in the German Baroque*

The 'Musica instrumentalis deudsch' of Martin Agricola

A treatise on musical instruments, 1529 and 1545

Translated and edited by

WILLIAM E. HETTRICK

Hofstra University

CAMBRIDGE
UNIVERSITY PRESS

Published by the Press Syndicate of the University of Cambridge
The Pitt Building, Trumpington Street, Cambridge CB2 1RP
40 West 20th Street, New York, NY 10011–4211, USA
10 Stamford Road, Oakleigh, Melbourne 3166, Australia

First published 1994

Printed in Great Britain at the University Press, Cambridge

A catalogue record for this book is available from the British Library

Library of Congress cataloguing in publication data
Agricola, Martin, 1486–1556.
[Musica instrumentalis deudsch. English]
The 'Musica instrumentalis deudsch' of Martin Agricola: a treatise
on musical instruments, 1529 and 1545;
translated and edited by William E. Hettrick.
p.   cm. – (Cambridge Musical Texts and Monographs)
Translation of the 1529 and 1545 editions.
Includes bibliographical references.
ISBN 0 521 36640 2 (hardback)
1. Musical instruments – Early works to 1800. 2. Music –
Theory – 16th century. I. Hettrick, William E. II. Title.
III. Series.
ML171.A26 1994
784 – dc20 93–11563 CIP

ISBN 0 521 36640 2 hardback

To the memory of Hans T. David
1902–1967

Contents

Preface

Because of their original purpose as textbooks, the published treatises of Martin Agricola exhibit a practical approach that makes them especially valuable today as sources of information about the study and performance of music in Germany in the first half of the sixteenth century. In fact, Agricola's entire life's work[1] was devoted to education. Born in the Silesian city of Schwiebus ca. 1486 as Martin Sore, he later changed his surname to the Latin word for farmer, an emphasis on peasant origins that was common among early Lutherans. His musical training is not documented, and – to judge from statements in several of his writings – he may have been largely self-taught in musical fundamentals, composition, singing and instrumental performance. By 1520 he is known to have arrived in Magdeburg (Saxony), an important early centre of Lutheran activity, where he worked as a music teacher and began his duties as Cantor at the Protestant municipal school sometime around the middle of the following decade. Agricola remained in Magdeburg for the rest of his remarkably productive life, teaching at the school, directing music at the Lutheran Church of St Ulrich, composing a body of polyphonic music based on chorales and plainchant and producing a number of treatises in German and Latin. He died in 1556.

Agricola's first publication, a textbook of musical fundamentals entitled *Ein kurtz deudsche Musica*,[2] was issued in 1528 from the press of Georg Rhau, the Wittenberg printer whose work was of great importance in the dissemination of Lutheran writings and music. Many of Agricola's succeeding books were also published by Rhau, and the author's dedications indicate a close professional relationship between the two men (although it was based solely on correspondence, as stated on fol. 5ᵛ of Agricola's dedication to the 1545 edition of *Musica instrumentalis deudsch*). The demand for copies of *Ein kurtz deudsche Musica* is shown by its subsequent editions with additional musical examples in 1529 and 1533. The last printing bears the new title *Musica choralis deudsch*, emphasising the subject of melodic modes and solmisation and implying a parallel with Agricola's other important treatises of that period (also printed by Rhau): *Musica instrumentalis deudsch* (1529), which champions the cause of instrumental music from both theological and practical standpoints, and *Musica figuralis deudsch* (1532), which deals with mensural notation and includes a separate short work on musical proportions entitled *Von den Proporcionibus*.[3]

Agricola's subsequent pedagogical and musical works generally reflect the tendency among Lutheran religious and educational leaders of the 1530s and 40s to return to the use of Latin in the German schools. Thus, in 1538, he produced an instructional book entitled *Scholia in musicam planam Venceslai Philomatis*, an expanded edition (with an appendix containing his own musical examples) of the *Musicorum libri quattuor* of Venceslaus Philomathes, originally published in Vienna in 1512 and probably known to Agricola through an edition issued by Georg Rhau in 1534.[4] The printer of Agricola's edition is not identified in surviving copies, but it may have been Michael Lotther of Magdeburg, who later printed Agricola's *Ein Sangbuchlein* [sic] *aller Sontags Evangelien* (1541), *Quaestiones vulgatiores in musicam* (1543) and *Musica ex prioribus a me aeditis musicis* (1547). Rhau printed Agricola's *Rudimenta musices, quibus canendi artificium compendiosissime complexum* (1539), and the posthumously published *Duo libri musices* (1561) was printed by Rhau's successors in Wittenberg.

The most popular book of Martin Agricola during his lifetime, and the one for which he is best known today, is his *Musica instrumentalis deudsch*, printed by Georg Rhau in 1529, 1530, 1532 and 1542, with an almost totally new edition appearing in 1545.[5] The title of the work presents an unmistakable allusion to the *Musica getutscht* of Sebastian Virdung, published in Basel in 1511.[6] The model for several subsequent treatises, Virdung's work is the first printed book on the subject of musical instruments as a whole, and it is especially valuable because the instruments are classified, discussed and illustrated in woodcuts. Virdung divides his subject into three categories (sig. A4ᵛ–C2ᵛ): instruments with strings (chordophones), those made to sound by wind (aerophones) and those made of metal or other sound-producing substance (idiophones). Included in the first category are the following subcategories: instruments with keyboards (clavichord, virginal, clavicimbalum, clavicytherium and hurdy-gurdy); those without keys, but with frets (lute, gittern and large fiddle (viol)); those without keys or frets, but with multiple courses of strings (harp, psaltery and dulcimer); and those – which he considers of no use – without keys or frets, and with only one or two strings (rebec and trumpet marine). Among the winds there are the following subcategories: instruments blown by human breath and having fingerholes (shawm, pommer, three-hole pipe, transverse flute, recorders, ruszpfeif, curved horn, gemshorn, cornett, crumhorns and bladderpipe); those blown by human breath and having no fingerholes (trombone, military trumpet, clareta and

tower trumpet; the bagpipe is illustrated along with these, but it would belong more properly to the first subcategory); and those blown by bellows (organ, positive organ, regal and portative organ). As examples of the third category of instruments, Virdung gives the anvil with hammers, bell and small bells. He then goes on (sig. C2ᵛ–D3ᵛ) to treat instruments attributed to St Jerome, as well as more practical percussion instruments. After presenting a number of folk instruments and introducing the method to be followed in the rest of his treatise (sig. D3ᵛ–E2), Virdung gives more specific information about the clavichord, the hexachordal system and the notation of music in both mensural style and keyboard tablature (sig. E2–I2). There follows a thorough discussion of the lute, including the selection and tuning of strings, the pitches available on the fingerboard and the notation of these pitches in traditional German lute tablature (sig. I2ᵛ–M3). Virdung concludes his treatise with a section on the recorder (sig. M3ᵛ–O4), giving instructions on fingering the treble, tenor and bass sizes, and presenting a number-tablature as a method for notating these instruments.

A direct connexion between *Musica getutscht* and the 1529 edition of *Musica instrumentalis deudsch* can be seen in the latter's many woodcut illustrations derived from Virdung's book. These were not printed from the original wood blocks, which were surely not accessible to Agricola and Rhau, but rather give every indication of having been copied free-hand from the earlier work, which served as a convenient source of usable pictures of musical instruments. In the process, Agricola's artist simplified or coarsened many of the details of the originals, rendering a number of the wind instruments, for example, with thinner profiles. He also reversed most of the original illustrations (probably the result of simply applying his drawings directly over the surfaces of the new wood blocks as patterns for cutting), although he was careful to retain the configurations of Virdung's harp and already-backwards keyboards, thus perpetuating the error in the latter case. Virdung's single illustrations of the transverse flute, viol and rebec were expanded to show four members of each family, but the earlier source's credible depiction of the relative dimensions of an ensemble of four recorders – showing, in fact, three sizes – was changed by Agricola's artist into a picture with only symbolic value, owing to his alteration of the instruments' proportions. Appendix 1 identifies the woodcuts in question and describes the major differences between the two sources.

Similarities in the texts of both works are also apparent, although Agricola's is couched in the form of verse[7] and exhibits some significant changes consistent with the practical nature of his book. Agricola follows Virdung's lead in setting up categories of musical instruments, but he changes the order of presentation, establishes somewhat different subcategories and gives more specific information related to performance. Agricola begins (chapters 1 and 2) with wind instruments, recognising two types: those with fingerholes (blown by human breath) and those without (whether blown by human breath or by bellows). Having thus broached the subject of organs in his treatment of the second type of wind instruments, he continues (chapter 3) with a presentation of mensural notation and keyboard tablature. Agricola's second category consists of string instruments, both those with keyboards (chapter 4) and those with fretted fingerboards (chapter 5). Within his discussion of the latter he ridicules the traditional German lute tablature, praises Lady Music, recounts the classical story of Arion's saving his own life through his musical ability, and presents a new, more logical notation for the lute similar to keyboard tablature. Chapter 6 continues the subject of lute tablature, showing methods for transcribing vocal notation, while chapter 7 deals with the selection and tuning of lute strings. Next come six chapters (8–13) devoted to bowed string instruments, which are given only cursory treatment by Virdung. Agricola presents three types of large and small fiddles having different numbers of strings and tunings (chapters 8–10) and gives a letter-tablature for all kinds of monophonic instruments (chapter 11). He then goes on to describe string instruments without keyboards or frets, but with many courses of strings (chapter 12) and those with only one, two or three strings (chapter 13), generally following Virdung in these classifications. Agricola ends his book (chapter 14) with his, and Virdung's, third category: instruments made of metal and other sound-producing substances. Here he expands Virdung's presentation to include the xylophone and, in connexion with the subject of the anvil and hammers, the classical account of the discovery of the proportions of weights and musical intervals by Pythagoras. In keeping with his avowed pedagogical emphasis in his book, Agricola omits portions of Virdung's work that would have had little practical application for his own readers: the pseudo-Jerome instruments, folk instruments and drums. Although both authors mention and illustrate brass instruments, neither has anything to say about playing them.

Agricola completely rewrote the main body of his text for the 1545 edition of *Musica instrumentalis deudsch*, claiming that the earlier version had been 'too obscure and difficult to understand' (fol. 3).[8] Most of the instruments presented in 1529 reappear in the 1545 edition, although some are changed in pitch and/or physical characteristics (flutes and fiddles), while others – evidently considered obsolete or otherwise not within the purview of the new edition – are either omitted entirely (rüspfeif, gemshorn, stringed keyboard instruments and smaller organs) or treated from a different standpoint (organ). As outlined below, much new information of a practical and scientific nature is added. While Agricola abandons his earlier method of classifying instruments strictly by category in favour of a looser organisation, he nevertheless generally follows the order established in the 1529 edition, starting with winds and continuing with strings and other instruments. These subjects are presented in long, somewhat rambling chapters, considerably fewer in number than in the earlier edition (five in 1545 as opposed to fourteen in 1529). This and other aspects of the 1545 edition suggest a lack of editorial supervision of its organisation. At any rate, the edition reflects the educational and religious climate in Saxony at the time of its publication, containing copious marginal notes, the use of Latin in many of these notes as well as in quotations within the text (perhaps in response to criticisms that his 1529 edition had lacked erudition), and extensive diatribes against the Roman Catholic Church. Agricola also refers to Martin Luther several times, including a timely citation of one of his tracts published in the very same year, 1545 (fol. 14).

Following prefatory material that includes a portrait of 'Lady Music', a preface and an address to the reader in the form of acrostics on 'MUSICA' and 'MARTINUS SORE', the first chapter of the 1545 edition (fols. 7–35) announces the subject of wind instruments but proceeds immediately with a second preface – longer than the first – advising the young reader to learn to sing, relating stories that describe the advantages of musical study in childhood, admonishing those who will not learn, praising Luther and other reformers, and dismissing Pope Paul III and his followers with scorn. Only after this lengthy discourse of

eighteen pages (fols. 7–15ᵛ)[9] does Agricola turn to the subject of the chapter, giving information on playing recorders, crumhorns, shawm, pommer, the small recorder with four holes and flutes. Inexplicably inserted between the presentations of two methods of notating the members of the flute family – and a telling example of the lack of organisation in this edition – is a two-page presentation of brass instruments (fols. 28ᵛ–29). Chapter 1 ends with a discussion of wind-instrument articulation (fols. 32–35), which reveals a practical knowledge on Agricola's part based probably on personal observation and perhaps also on actual playing experience.

Chapter 2 (fols. 35–51ᵛ) concerns bowed strings, and Agricola first discusses the note-values that receive separate bows and the symbols used in letter-tablature. Next come the tunings of the various instruments and the setting of frets on the fingerboards (fols. 36ᵛ–51). The chapter ends with an epilogue (fol. 51ᵛ) in which the method of ornamentation employed by organists is briefly recommended.

The lute and monochord are dealt with in chapter 3 (fols. 52–65), beginning with the positions of the frets and the selection and tuning of the lute strings. With respect to the monochord, Agricola gives a thorough presentation of the location of pitches along the string according to the Pythagorean intervals. Chapter 4 (fols. 65ᵛ–78) treats the Pythagorean system further, recounting the traditional story of the discovery of the weights of hammers and the resulting musical intervals and proportions, quoting from Macrobius's Latin account of the subject, presenting methods of adding and subtracting proportions, listing the proportions related to some forty-four intervals, and applying this information to the determination of dimensions of organ pipes and weights of bells.

By comparison with the first four chapters, the fifth is so short as to appear to be an afterthought (fols. 78ᵛ–80ᵛ). Here Agricola covers the remaining topics contained in chapter 14 of the 1529 edition (having already presented a greatly expanded discussion of the Pythagorean proportions) – the harp, psaltery and xylophone – adding also the dulcimer. Agricola ends his book with a reiteration of his claim of being self-taught, a final condemnation of his attackers, a request that his students persuade their parents to raise his salary, a promise to publish some instrumental pieces and a prayer for long life.

Altogether, twenty-three surviving copies of the 1529 edition of *Musica instrumentalis deudsch* are documented.[10] In addition to the diplomatic edition of Robert Eitner,[11] four of these copies were consulted in the preparation of the present translation. They are listed below, along with sigla by which they will be identified hereafter:

A   Augsburg (Germany), Staats- und Stadtbibliothek
F   Flensburg (Germany), Bibliothek des staatlichen Gymnasiums[12]
H   Harvard University, Cambridge, Mass. (USA), Houghton Library
N   New York, N.Y. (USA), New York Public Library

An examination of these four copies alone has revealed discrepancies that point to a complicated printing history of the 1529 edition – undoubtedly the result of the large demand for this first edition of the book, to which the reprintings in 1530, 1532 and 1542 also attest. A full treatment of this history lies beyond the purview of the present volume, but as a first step in this study the major differences among the four copies in question are cited here in notes. In the case of the 1545 edition, two copies were consulted in addition to the Eitner edition: they are located in Augsburg, Staats- und Stadtbibliothek, and Wolfenbüttel (Germany), Herzog August Bibliothek.[13] Except for missing leaves, very few discrepancies have been found between these two copies; they are likewise cited here in notes.

By far the most ephemeral parts of the two editions of Agricola's treatise have proved to be the foldouts containing diagrams, no doubt for the practical reason that as separate, over-sized sheets they were easily lost before the individual volumes were bound. In fact, among the four copies of the 1529 edition consulted, only A has the three foldouts that belong to the volume (cited on fols. 25ᵛ, 37ᵛ and 42ᵛ, the first two foldouts containing two diagrams each). They are missing entirely in the three other copies, including F, as presented in the facsimile published by Georg Olms Verlag (1969). The Wolfenbüttel copy of the 1545 edition has all three of that volume's foldouts (cited on fols. 59, 63ᵛ and 75ᵛ), while the first one is missing in the Augsburg copy.

The Augsburg copies of both editions serve as the source of almost all the material presented here in facsimile. The only exceptions to this are four pages taken from the Wolfenbüttel copy of the 1545 edition: fols. 23ᵛ, 34 and 34ᵛ (providing better pictures than the Augsburg copy) and the foldout cited on fol. 59 (missing in the Augsburg copy). Thanks are hereby expressed to the officials of these two libraries for permission to reproduce this material.

Although the Eitner edition has many flaws, especially in the completely redrawn illustrations, it remains the only published edition that contains the full contents of both editions of *Musica instrumentalis deudsch*. Moreover, it is relatively accessible, being found in most major research libraries, either in its original version of 1896 or in the reprint by Broude Brothers (1966). For these reasons the present translation has been designed to allow the reader to use the Eitner edition as a diplomatic source of the original text. All of its textual errors are cited here in notes; the numerous mistakes in its illustrations are not cited, however, because facsimiles of the original woodcuts are provided here (the reader is advised to be highly sceptical of all the illustrations in the Eitner edition).

The present translation reproduces the original layout of both editions of Agricola's treatise with respect to facing verso and recto pages, which are placed here side by side on each page. Foldouts cited in the text are given here as appendices, which also include editorial tables and transcriptions of many of Agricola's diagrams. All original illustrative material is reproduced here (except for symbols used to indicate the intended placement of the foldouts), and all textual material is accounted for, including running heads and marginal notes; catchwords at the bottoms of pages are omitted, however. Consecutive folio numbers are printed in the upper right corners of most recto pages in both original editions (predominantly roman numerals in the 1529 edition and arabic numerals in the 1545 edition). These provide the basis for the editorial folio numbers (all given as arabic numerals) supplied here in the headings of all recto and verso pages. All references to original pages in the present study make use of these folio numbers. Some other studies cite only signature marks, however, and as an aid to readers that system of pagination is also supplied here editorially. Agricola's 1529 edition comprises eight signatures, with the first seven (A–G) all having a full group of eight folios each, and the last (H) having only four. The 1545 edition is made up of eleven signatures, with the first nine (A–I) having eight folios each, the next (K) having four, and the last (L)

having eight (the last folio being blank). Folios 6, 7 and 8 in each signature are not marked, and many of the first five folios likewise bear no mark.

While running heads are found on most of the pages of Agricola's 1545 edition and follow a regular pattern in the main, those of the 1529 edition are less consistently applied, and many pages lack them altogether. In fact, three pages of the earlier edition have running heads stating incorrect chapter numbers that are one too low in each case (fols. 27, 48 and 51^v); these are translated here as they appear in the original.

Translations of the original marginal notes are supplied here – mingled with editorial notes in a common numbering series for each section of the book – and are identified in each case by the prefatory designation '*in margin*'. The location of each marginal note in the text is indicated by the appropriate superscript numeral placed directly after the word that begins the poetic line closest to the position of the note in the original. In the case of prose text, the numeral is placed after the most appropriate word in the corresponding line.

Translations of text within the illustrative material reproduced here in facsimile are given in parentheses directly underneath that material, and the relative positions of the words in question are indicated, where necessary, by prefatory designations that make use of the following words: '*top*', '*upper*', '*middle*', '*lower*' and '*bottom*' to describe the vertical dimension, and '*left*', '*centre*' and '*right*' to describe the horizontal. Unless otherwise reported, a vertical series of words or phrases (usually referred to as a '*column*') is translated in the order of top to bottom, and a horizontal series (usually indicated as '*across . . .*') is translated from left to right.

Because the editorial transcriptions of musical examples

included here retain the original note-values, the traditional names for these values have been retained (translated into English forms where appropriate) for the sake of consistency. They are the following: maxima, long, breve, semibreve (whole-note), minim (half-note), semiminim (crotchet, quarter-note), fusa (quaver, eighth-note) and semifusa (semiquaver, sixteenth-note).

All of the pitches cited in this translation are to be understood as representing the original written notation, regardless of any transposition that may be necessary in order to apply this notation to the ranges of certain instruments. Because pitch names are used extensively in both editions of Agricola's treatise, not only appearing in the text but also integrated into the diagrams (many of which are reproduced here in facsimile), the original symbols have been retained. Appendix 2 identifies them and shows all of their forms found in the two editions. In editorial discussions of fingering positions on the necks of string instruments, each intersection of string (or course) and fret is abbreviated here by means of a symbol showing the pitch of the former and the number of the latter. Thus, '**g**:0' means open **g** string; '**g**:1' means **g** string, first fret; and so on.

In both editions of *Musica instrumentalis deudsch*, Agricola presents the body of his text in the form of rhymed German couplets. With some exceptions, these are made up of lines of ten syllables in the 1529 version and lines of eight syllables in the 1545 version. Whether or not this poetic treatment actually resulted in greater understanding and retention on the part of his young sixteenth-century readers, as Agricola avows in his preface to the 1529 edition (fol. 2ᵛ), the resulting verse of dubious literary quality certainly increases the work of the modern translator. Many of Agricola's end-words seem superfluous (and some of those most commonly used appear in a variety of spellings),

evidently having been chosen more for the sake of rhyme than for the purpose of achieving clarity or elegance of style. At least a portion of the resulting redundant and even naive effect must necessarily be carried over into the translation. In many places it is difficult to determine where one thought ends and the next begins; punctuation is not always helpful in this regard, as it is mostly used not to indicate meaning but simply to demarcate the ends of rhymed couplets. As is the case with any translation, certain words in the original German could not be rendered as a single word throughout in the English text. *Kunst*, for example, has a number of meanings (art, skill, knowledge, science), and the appropriate interpretation of the word has been chosen here in each context. Another example is *Pfeiff(e)*, which has been translated here variously as 'recorder', 'flute', 'woodwind', 'wind instrument' or simply 'instrument', according to context. Unless they are identical to their English forms, all names of musical instruments and other important musical terms in the original text are included here in square brackets at their first appearance and at significant subsequent points. Certain idiomatic passages, especially proverbs, have been translated freely in order to give the best effect. To cite just two examples, *Ein alt hund wird schwerlich bendig gemacht* and *mit hend und füss weren* (both found on fol. 12ᵛ of the 1545 edition) are rendered here, respectively, as 'An old dog cannot be taught new tricks' and 'to fight tooth and nail' rather than the literal 'An old dog is difficult to make obedient' and 'to fight with hands and feet'.

All abbreviations in the original text are spelt out here in full, mostly without notice although significant examples are cited in the notes. Uses of the word *Musica* in the original to personify the goddess of music are capitalised here.

At this point it is my pleasant duty to acknowledge the

assistance I have received in the preparation of the present study. Hofstra University supported my work in the form of a grant for the purchase of microfilms from the Faculty Research Fund of Hofstra College of Liberal Arts and Sciences and a teaching-load reduction from the Center for Scholarly Research and Academic Excellence. In this context I particularly want to thank Dr Robert C. Vogt, Dean of Hofstra College of Liberal Arts and Sciences, and Dr Edgar E. Dittemore, Chairman of the Music Department, for their support. I also wish to express my gratitude to Dr Margaret A. Schatkin (Boston College), who assisted ably with the identification of some of the Latin quotations, as well as their translation; Dr Raymond N. Greenwell (Hofstra University), who helped me considerably with the mathematical parts of my work; Dr Beth Bullard (Dickinson College), who kindly provided me with a typescript copy of her translation of *Musica getutscht*; Mrs Penny Souster, Ms Lucy Carolan and their colleagues at Cambridge University Press, who expertly guided the production of this volume; and especially my wife, Dr Jane Schatkin Hettrick (Rider College), who helped me immeasurably with the idiomatic translation of Agricola's version of early New High German and was always ready to give her support and encouragement. Finally, I want to acknowledge my great debt to the late Howard Mayer Brown, who first suggested that I undertake this project, continued to give me valuable comments and suggestions, and indeed brought his editorial guidance to completion just prior to his untimely death.

Early in the course of my work on the present study I toyed with the idea of translating Agricola's poetic text entirely into English verse, expanding my earlier publication of the sections on woodwinds from the two editions of his treatise.[14] I decided, however, that although such a presentation might prove entertaining to the reader, it would only substitute inevitably doggerel English poetry for the original German verses of similar quality, and therefore could not serve the requirements of scholarship as well as the plain prose translation that has ensued. Nevertheless, to conclude this preface, perhaps I may be permitted to quote my own versified rendering[15] of four lines written by Agricola in defence of his work (1529 edition, fol. 12ᵛ):

Was ligt mir denn dran
Ich hab es gethan.
Und ein mal gewagt
Wie manche schöne magd.

What I planned for this book
I've accomplished; I took
One big risk, I confess,
Like a girl who said 'Yes'!

Instrumental Music in German
[*Musica instrumentalis deudsch*],

in which is included how one is to learn various kinds of wind
instruments [*Pfeiffen*] from vocal notation [*nach dem gesange*], and
also how it is to be transcribed into the correctly established
tablature for the organ [*Orgel*], harp [*Harffen*], lute [*Lauten*],
fiddle [*Geigen*] and all kinds of keyboard and string instruments
[*Instrument und Seytenspiel*].

Martin Agricola

Grace and peace of God to readers

Previously I also had a German Music[1] published in which a brief method and model for easily learning to sing was clearly and simply written down for young people. For it is surely quite essential and is in truth very necessary for young people who are first beginning to learn not to be overwhelmed and frightened off by many useless words and rules, but instead to be enticed and stimulated to study, diligently taught through brief, clear instruction and introduction to the art. Also, just as neither solid food, nor all kinds of it, nor too much of it will be good at first for a young child who is supposed to learn to eat (rather, some soft grain mush must be spread out for him, and a little mashed egg prechewed, so that he learns

to eat and gets used to food), thus it will also be the case with none other than those who are first beginning to learn something (it makes no difference in which art it may be), that one should present them with the principal elements, the foundation, the correct fundamentals and the essence of the art in the briefest and easiest way, and then indeed let them learn these things. Therefore, out of heartfelt Christian love and kind intentions, which we all owe to each other, I have published the second part of Music, which is called Instrumental Music, and which teaches how to play all kinds of stringed keyboard instruments [*auf allerley Instrument*], organs, lutes, harps, fiddles, wind instruments and the like, accordingly as God has granted me grace, in the briefest and simplest German, brought forth – together with their correct method and tablature – into a small book for the great advantage and benefit of young people and all others devoted to this noble art, including laymen and nonspecialists who only know how to read. I have written this in German rhyme and metre for a particular reason: so that young people and others who might want to learn this art can comprehend it all the more easily and retain it all the longer. For experience teaches that fine epigrams and proverbs that rhyme are much more easily understood and remain fresh in the memory longer than those that are expressed in a plain manner without rhymes. But if there are some people who do not consider this reason sufficient or for any other reason would not like this book, I want to have implored them, in a kind and purposeful way, to look in a Christian manner on my sincere good will and intentions of being straightforward and useful to poor young people in the matter of this praiseworthy art, and to put the best construction on my finished endeavour (as is fair, after all), and to think on the saying, 'It is easy to criticise a thing, but very difficult to make it better.'

Martin Agricola

To Georg Rhau, bookprinter in Wittenberg, I, Martin Agricola, wish the grace and peace of God.

Kind, dear lord Jörg,[2] since in my first book of German Music, dedicated to you, I committed myself and promised to send you also an Instrumental Music and let it be published by you, I consider it not only meet and right, but also necessary, to make good my pledge and promise. The first reason is so that I might not be scolded by you for being a good-for-nothing who promises much but delivers little. The second is because there are many who are highly celebrated and well skilled in this art, but few indeed who, out of brotherly Christian love and equity, make this aforementioned noble art public or bring it out in print for the sake of their neighbours and of young people; and then they get only grief from it (as I have indeed experienced several times). This may happen solely out of envy and hate, out of hostile intentions and a haughty heart, so that they alone might have public fame and glory and be considered famous and important because they know something special that others do not know. For this reason they also say, 'Art must be held back, so that art will endure.' When one expresses oneself in this manner, it may well give an illusion and a good appearance to the world, but to God it is truly unchristian, indeed quite heathen talk; and I look forward to seeing how they will fare at the Last Judgement, when God will say to them, 'I have graced you with great art, with particular understanding, and I have heaped riches on you, so that through them you would serve your neighbour and communicate these things. But you have kept them for yourselves and have used them for your own pleasure, fame

and pride.' Then they will surely see what kind of excuse and apology it is to say, 'Art must be held back, so that art will endure.' In order that, now for the second time, I might present, to people who are highly celebrated and greatly learned in this art, a Christian example and model for helping young people (since I am considered a minor musician, practised in this art, although unworthy), and so that I might make good the promise I made to you, dear lord Jorg, I am sending you this same Instrumental Music, together with many new methods and tablatures for instruments, requesting kindly that your love and favour will receive it (like the previous one) thankfully under your protection and patronage – first, to issue it from your press with care and diligence in the best way, and then to help to defend, guard and protect it faithfully from filthy, shameful and hateful slanderers. Given at Magdeburg on St Bartholomew's Day, [24 August] 1528.

Martin Agricola

Concerning the description of
instrumental music, how many categories
it is divided into, and what types each
category contains.

The first chapter

I will show here, briefly, the description of this kind of Music.
It is an art that directs us how to take instruments in hand and
employ them with dexterity. Some of them are written about
here.

It is divided into three categories, as I will now correctly
instruct you.

The first category of musical instruments, which are made to sound and are blown solely by means of wind, since they have hollow pipes [*hole rören*].

The first category of these instruments is made properly with
hollow pipes and blown very artfully by means of wind; it is
of two types, as it seems to me.

Some are blown by human breath, according to the
present usage, and they are also found to be of two types.
Some are bored with fingerholes, through which the sound
and melody are freely channelled and measured out: for
example, recorders [*Flöten*], cornetts [*Zincken*], pommers
[*Bomhart*], shawms [*Schalmeyn*], crumhorns [*Kromhörner*],
transverse flutes [*Querfeiffen*], and also three-hole pipes
[*Schwegel*], small recorders [*klein Flöt*], bladderpipes [*Platerspiel*] and bagpipes [*Sackpfeiffen*] – all must be played by means
of fingerholes. Do not forget gemshorns [*Ziegen hörner*] and
rüspfeiffs [*Rüspfeiff*],[3] for they are considered similar to the
above. I will choose some of these and give a lesson on them,
as follows.

How a wind instrument [*pfeiffe*] is first taken into the hands.

Take up the wind instrument for the very first time in both
hands, and you may have the choice of which hand you want
to hold on top; the other should always hold sway below.
Next, place each finger into its position on its hole, in
appropriate order. To begin with, the one for the little finger
of the lower hand is called the first; the others are as they
follow one by one and are identified with numbers below.
Also, you should always plug up the unfingered hole nearby
[at the bottom] with wax. Now if you hold the instrument
according to the following depiction, you will give your
playing a correct appearance.

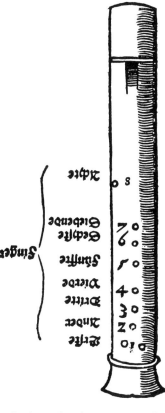

Always close up the first unfingered[4] hole on the other side with wax.

(*Left column, from bottom:* Finger: first; second; third; fourth; fifth; sixth; seventh; eighth.)

A fine and correctly established foundation for learning to play correctly from vocal music and notation [*nach dem gesange und den Noten*] on recorders, crumhorns, cornetts, pommers, shawms and bagpipes, and how they are to be fingered correctly.

If you want to comprehend the correct foundation for playing recorders and crumhorns skilfully, and cornetts, pommers and shawms with artfulness, then observe the following at all times.

If you want to master the correct foundation, then vocal music will bring you great benefit. With instruments it is the case that whoever understands vocal music can, by himself, comprehend and learn more with his effort in half a quarter of a year (if he applies himself) than one who is not experienced with vocal music can accumulate in a half-year, for Music is the foundation from which all instruments proceed. Therefore, if you derive your fundamentals from this art, you will reap great advantage. And if you practise both aspects [i.e., fingering and reading notation] diligently, you should be able to attain all kinds of skill. For there is nothing so difficult on earth that cannot be acquired with diligence. Now I shall speak further and inform you of the unchanging method of these diagrams, which plainly shows the practice of wind instruments and the way to apply the fingers correctly.

First, you must strive very hard to understand what[5] the numbers and circles indicate. The filled-in circle means all holes closed; in[6] the bass this makes **FF** under Γ, in[7] the treble [*Discant*] **G**.[8] Pay attention diligently, and do not think of this as a trifle. The[9] open circle indicates all holes uncovered; if you blow into the unfingered instrument [*in die Pfeiff an abelan*] in just the same way, you[10] will have **G** in the bass, **d** in the tenor and **aa** in the treble (believe this for a fact). Pay heed also to the written numbers, for (I say) they also have great authority. Each one refers indeed to a finger, which is raised up from its hole: 1 indicates the first finger and 2 the second, as the diagram proves to everyone. I will teach you in one example to understand the other numbers, for any purpose. Thus,[11] the highest position but one in the diagram and elsewhere signifies indeed the first, second, third and fourth fingers, and also the eighth moved halfway off the hole.[12] This[13] fingering produces **c**[14] for a bass player, **g** in the tenor and **dd** in the treble – which can easily be understood from the illustrated hands and instruments, as follows. Thus, always be mindful of the numbers, below, above, in the middle and everywhere. Also, if you want to play woodwind instruments [*das Pfeiffenwerk*] correctly, then let the other fingers remain in place

(those that are not indicated by numbers) and the instrument will sound proper and fine. Also, when you want to lift up your fingers, let them hover over the holes; each one is to remain near its hole so that it will not come down incorrectly. Understand the letters with tittles [i.e., added signs] as[15] indicating chromatic notes [*Musica ficta*]. **C**♯ requires **D**♭; **D**♯, **E**♭; **F**♯ shows us **G**♭; **G**♯, **A**♭ – as can be found, apparent and clear, in the diagrams written below. Finally, you should take heed diligently that you do not blow the instrument the way peasants do.[16] Apply your tongue to all the notes, whether eight or four of them go in one bar [*schlag*]. I will not speak of ornaments [*Mordanten*], although they make music elegant. If you want to use them in this activity, then you can learn them by observing a piper. I will therefore let this stand now and not write any more about it at this time, for the text and the following diagrams can guide and direct everyone to be able, artfully and in a short time, to comprehend the abovementioned wind instruments correctly and with quick cunning – unless he has a very low intelligence.

Furthermore, cornetts, crumhorns and recorders all follow one practice in fingering. Bagpipes also belong with these, as well as others that one perceives to be the same.

Crumhorns[17] do not go any higher, however, than the eight uncovered holes. Therefore not every piece is suitable for them that fits on recorders and large wind instruments [*gros Pfeifen*]. Because of this, if I have the opportunity, I plan (as I am able) to write music for every wind instrument, so that one dare not laugh out of scorn; for when recorder music is played on crumhorns and is fingered incorrectly, as often happens through mutation [*Mutirn*; i.e., shifting from one hexachord to another], and many errors are committed, much derision often befalls many a poor lad when things do not sound right. Therefore play correctly in a proper manner, although you may still be scoffed at many times.

Furthermore,[18] there have been some who have gathered numbers together and have created a tablature for wind instruments,[19] which others consider a fraud. I will also give my own opinion of it, which everyone can bear and endure. If you want to intabulate something from vocal notation (for the aforementioned wind instruments and others on which one part is played), then I advise you to follow the method

that[20] is referred to below concerning fiddles [*Geigen*],[21] and you will not easily be led astray. But it is much better and quite suitable for[22] such monophonic instruments to be played from vocal notation; in this way no one need be distressed because of the exertion [of making a separate tablature]. For if I were to have to transcribe something out of necessity, I would become vexed very quickly. Therefore, when playing a wind instrument, it is very much easier to read a part from notes than to play from tablature; you only have to practise. Now you may say, 'That is too hard for me, for I really don't know vocal notation at all.' But, dear fellow, practice makes perfect; where this is lacking, everything is in vain. You ought to have this lesson from me. If you think you know better, then you may run along.

There follows the correct foundation for the abovementioned wind instruments, quite masterfully contained in three diagrams.[23]

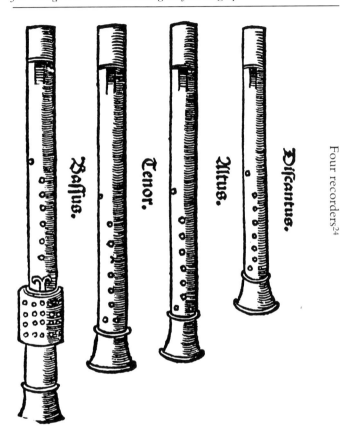

(Bass. Tenor. Alto. Treble.)

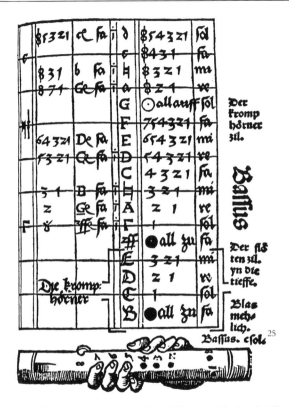

(*Lower left:* Crumhorns. *Right column:* All open. All closed. All closed. *Far-right column:* The crumhorn limit. Bass. The bottom recorder limit. Blow gradually. [The fingering for] bass **c**.)

[See Appendix 3 for a composite transcription of the fingering charts for recorders and related instruments on fols. 9, 9ᵛ and 10.]

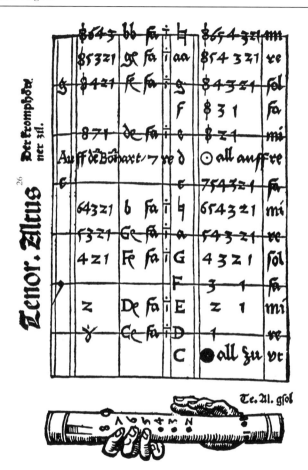

(*Far-left column:* The crumhorn limit. Tenor-alto. *Middle left:* On the pommer. *Right column:* All open. All closed. [The fingering for] tenor-alto **g**.

(*Middle left:* Shawm. *Right column:* All open. All closed. [The fingering for] treble **dd**. *Far-right column:* The crumhorn limit. Treble.)

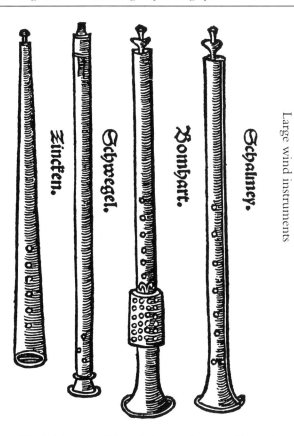

Zincken.
Schwegel.
Bombart.
Schalmey.

Large wind instruments

([Straight] cornett. Three-hole pipe. Pommer. Shawm.)

Vier Kromphörner/oder Pfeiffen.

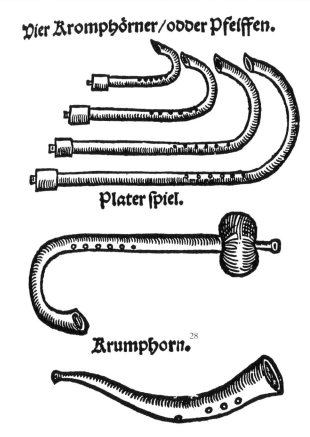

Plater spiel.

Krumphorn. [28]

(Four crumhorns. Bladderpipe. Curved horn.)

Gemſen horn.[29]   **Rüſpfeyff.**

Sackpfeiff.

(*Top:* Gemshorn. Rüspfeiff. *Bottom:* Bagpipe.)

A second fine and correct foundation, showing how three or four Swiss flutes [*Schweitzerpfeiffen*] are employed together according to the demands of the music, and how the six holes are to be fingered correctly according to the written notes.

Further, I will instruct you well with this diagram how to finger the notes properly, one by one, on a Swiss or transverse flute [*Querpfeiffen*]. You should understand the[30] numbers and circles as they are shown in connexion with recorders, but there is another method of blowing, as the diagrams now show. Blow[31] the lowest eight notes very moderately; let[32] the next seven be somewhat faster; the[33] next four require a faster breath; and[34] the highest three go very quickly. Also, if you want to master the fundamentals and basics, then learn to play with quivering breath, for it graces the music very much on all wind instruments that one plays. But I will now let this stand; you can produce it yourself with practice, for it is not considered of much use to chatter a lot about something, but teach little. Therefore we will continue the discussion and, in three finely drawn diagrams, reveal the correct foundation, which proceeds gradually out of correct practice. And I hope that every intelligent man will easily be able to comprehend, from the diagrams, how each one is to be understood – that is, unless he is unable to count up to three. In that case, I truly cannot advise him; he may as well eat a well-roasted turnip and wish to become more intelligent from it, for only then would he amount to something in this world. A word to the wise is sufficient, but there will be many who are not pleased with it. What matters to me in this, I have done, and I have taken a risk just once, like many a fair maiden.

In the following diagrams, see how you are to finger the holes on the Swiss flute in the proper manner.

Baſſus. Tenor. Altus. Diſcantus.

Four Swiss flutes[35]

(Bass. Tenor. Alto. Treble.)

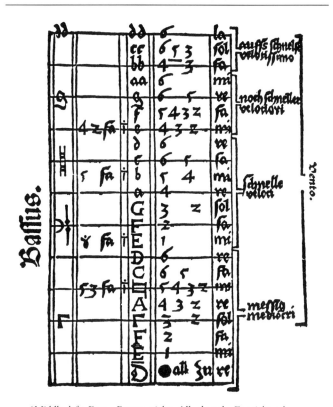

(*Middle left:* Bass. *Bottom right:* All closed. *Far-right column:* Wind: the fastest; faster; fast; moderate.)

[See Appendix 4 for a composite transcription of the fingering charts for Swiss flutes on fols. 13ᵛ, 14 and 14ᵛ.]

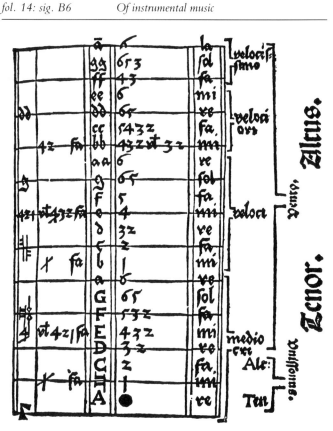

(*Right column:* Wind: fastest; faster; fast; moderate. Unison: alto; tenor. *Far-right column:* Alto. Tenor.)

Discantus.

(*Middle left:* Treble. *Far-right column:* Wind: fastest; faster; fast; moderate.)

A fine foundation, to be learnt on a small recorder [*klein Flötlein*] that has no more than four holes, except that when the lowest end of the instrument is also employed (as commonly happens), it may be reckoned as having five or six holes.

Further, I do not wish to omit, but rather to broach the subject of the practice of the small recorder and how the holes are to be fingered correctly and cleverly. First pick up the instrument in the right hand, or in the left without any disgrace.[36] Your other hand will be free and independent, except that you control the bottom hole [i.e., the open end of the instrument] solely with the finger next to the thumb [i.e., the index finger], as shown in the diagram.

In this diagram, the bottom end of the instrument is also reckoned as a hole or note when it is half-fingered, as follows.

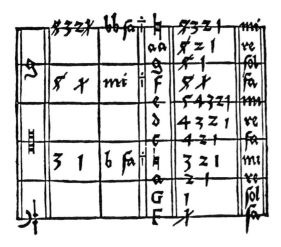

[See Appendix 5 for a transcription of this fingering chart for the small recorder with four holes.]

Klein Flötlin mit vier löchern

(Small recorder with four holes.)

The second type of instruments in the first category: namely, wind instruments that can be blown by human breath and have no fingerholes, as follows.

Some instruments, however, have no holes – just one at the top and one at the bottom, through which the melody is produced solely and completely by blowing and drawing [a slide]. Examples are the trombone [*Busaun*], trumpets [*Trumeten*] and clareta [*Claret*],[37] as shown here in the following illustration. I shall not say much about them at this time, for I do not yet possess the proper fundamentals; but when I obtain them, you will receive them correctly from me. Nevertheless, in order not to let this merely pass, I will show pictures of them to you.[38]

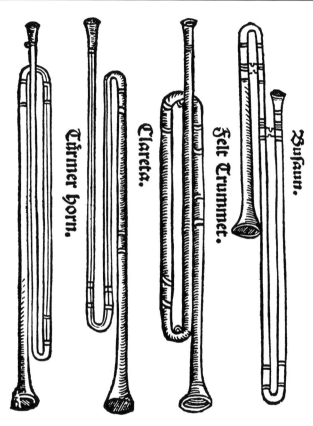

(Tower trumpet. Clareta. Military trumpet. Trombone.)

The second type of instruments in the first category, which are blown not by human breath, but by bellows (as follows).

The second chapter

The second type of hollow pipes [*rören*] in the first category is, at this time, that which is not blown by human breath. They are all instruments, as I tell you, that produce a sound by means of bellows. Examples are the organ [*Orgel*], positive [*Posityff*], regal, portative [*Portatyff*] and others considered to be similar, whose sound is made by means of bellows. I will also draw on something from this subject when[39] I begin the matter of transcribing. No more of this here, but look at their forms, as they are correctly pictured below.

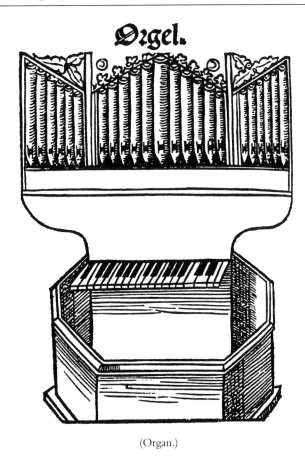

(Organ.)

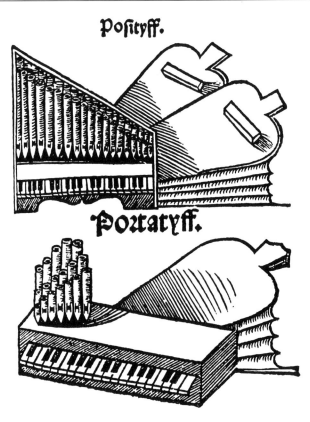

(Positive. Portative.)

(Regal.)

How to transcribe music from vocal notation into letter notation or tablature for all kinds of instruments on which three or four parts are played.

The third chapter

For anyone who wants to transcribe something into tablature and then enjoy it on the organ or other similar instruments, I say graciously that it is necessary for him to know (as I say) at least how many notes go in one beat [*schlag*], and also how to form their shapes [*ihr art*] correctly and change them into their letters. Then (I advise) he should not forget how they are measured by means of little flags [*hecklein*] [attached to the stems]. Next, he must pay attention diligently to the clefs [*schlusseln*; i.e., letters] by which the notes are indicated, whether they are made large or small, and whether they have a tittle [i.e., a line] below or above them. Music teaches this in her scale [*leyter*]; look there for it, and enquire further.

There follows: how one is to recognise the differences among letters [*buchstaben*] in the musical scale.[40]

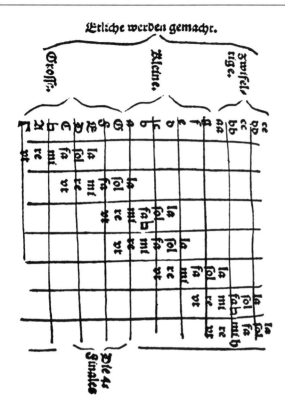

(*Across the top:* Some are made: large; small; double. *Bottom:* The 4 finals.)

The scale of the five written clefs[41]

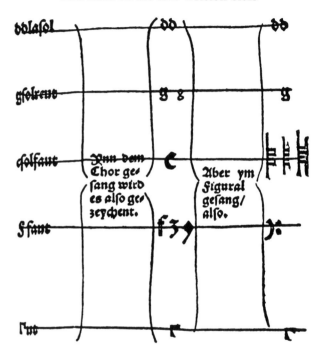

(*Middle left:* In plainchant these are written thus. *Middle right:* But in polyphonic music, thus.)

These five clefs are all found on lines, and each stands a 5th apart from the other, except that the Γ stands a 7th below **F**.

Concerning three differences among clefs or letters, and how they are employed in transcribing music into tablature.

If you are to become acquainted with transcribing, then set the double letters in the treble as small letters but indeed with lines above them. The large letters in the bass (believe this for a fact) are at times also made small, except that they are provided with tittles [i.e., lines] underneath, as the following diagram shows. Observe it well, and you will be praised.

Thus the double letters[42]

aa bb ♭ h cc ᴅᴅ ee ff gg.

are[43] made as follows when transcribing into tablature:

[letter forms]

The[44] small letters are made:

a b ♮ h c ᴅ e f g.

The large letters are made:[45]

[letter forms]

or[46] as follows:[47]

[letter forms]

How the notes and little flags [attached to the stems] over the letters are made in transcribing, and what they mean.

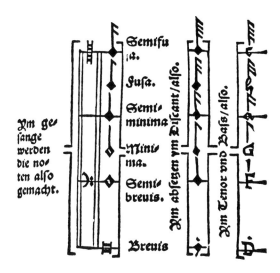

(*Left:* In vocal notation the notes are made thus. *Centre column:* Semifusa. Fusa. Semiminim. Minim. Semibreve. Breve. *Right:* In transcribing, thus in the treble. *Far right:* Thus in the tenor and bass.)

Although I have considered here only how the treble is made with notes and the other voices with letters, nevertheless I should also tell you that often all the voices altogether are notated entirely in letters. If everyone does this as he pleases, then his intention will be satisfied.

What is useful to know about ligatures, or notes bound together, in transcribing.

Also, if you want to investigate transcribing, you must know about ligatures, which are notes bound together, as I will briefly show you below, well composed in several rules. May God give no good fortune to him who hates this.

The names and forms of the notes in polyphonic music[48]

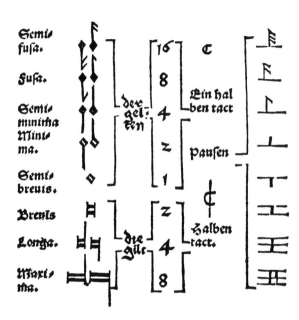

(*Far-left column:* Semifusa. Fusa. Semiminim. Minim. Semi-breve. Breve. Long. Maxima. *Across the upper middle:* Of these, [the given number] equal a half-bar. *Middle right:* Rests. *Across the lower middle:* [Each of] these equals [the given number of] half-bars.)

Only in the simple notes is the stem [*schwantz*] directed up and down; in the ligatures there is another method, which you will be taught here, as follows.

The value of each note, in common symbols, as follows

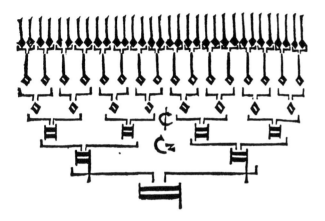

A preface concerning ligatures

Since it often happens in vocal notation that separate notes are not used and one finds not just one, but rather three or four notes bound together, and because not everyone understands all of them, I have been motivated, as is proper, to indicate to the inexperienced correctly and quickly (as every true fellow ought to do) what [the notes in] ligatures mean, whether they are placed at the beginning, the middle or the end.

What a ligature is

A ligature is, if you want to get to the bottom of it, a binding together of two or more notes by means of appropriate little lines, by which they are drawn together.

The four notes that can be bound

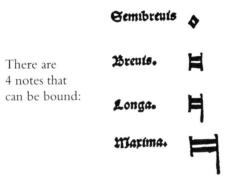

There are 4 notes that can be bound:

(Semibreve. Breve. Long. Maxima.)

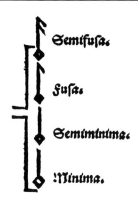

These cannot be bound; therefore they are neither found nor sung in ligatures:

(Semifusa. Fusa. Semiminim. Minim.)

About two forms of ligatures

Every ligature in the world can be made in two shapes. The first is described as exactly square; the second has an oblique form [*eine kromme gestalt*].

Concerning the first notes of ligatures

The first rule

A first note without a stem is in truth a long if indeed the second descends below it.[49]

The second rule

A first note without a stem is called a breve if the second ascends directly after it.[50]

The third rule

A first note with a stem descending from the left always wants to be a breve.[51]

The fourth rule

When the stem of the first note goes up on the left side, then the note is a semibreve, along with the second.[52]

Concerning the middle notes

The first rule

All notes written between the first and the last are considered middle notes.

The second rule

Every note situated in the middle is assessed by singers as a breve, except that when the first note has an [ascending] stem, then it and the second note are semibreves, as is reported above in the fourth rule. Observe this in all the rules set down below.[53]

The middle notes are breves.

Concerning the final notes

The first rule

If a final square note [*quadrat*] descends, it is identified as a long.[54]

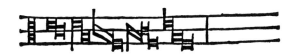

Let a final descending square note be a long for you.

The second rule

If a final square note is written ascending, then it is counted as a breve.[55]

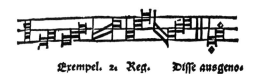

(Example of the second rule. With the exception of these.)

The third rule

Every final oblique note [*Obliqua*] is a breve; it is all the same whether it goes up or down.[56]

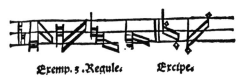

(Example of the third rule. Make an exception.)

The final rule

The maxima, because it is the largest note, always remains in its basic form.[57]

Examples of the maxima.

Instructions for transcribing [into tablature]

If you now have an understanding of all of this, then first take the treble and write it in vocal notation, as follows. Notate it on five or six lines, making sure that each whole beat [*gantzer schlag*] always stands separate from the next, so that it will come to you all the more easily and will be judged of good quality by everyone. Then transcribe the tenor from notes into letters (let this be said to you) so that all of the beats [*schleg*] of the tenor fall directly under the beats [*Tact*] of the treble. Finally, [transcribe] the bass also into letters, and hear what you are to do with it: notate it with its beats [*Tact*], as I indicate, under the beats [*schlege*] of the tenor and treble, as I will show you in the diagram. If you observe it, then you will be praised. You can employ such an intabulation, I say to you quickly, for all instruments on which more than one voice is realised, whether they have a keyboard or not. However, the lute has another form [of tablature], which will be reported in the sixth chapter.

There follows a diagram showing how the notes and rests are written. [See Appendices 6–8.]

The second category of musical instruments, which are strung with strings and therefore are called string instruments [*Seytenspiel*], as follows.

The fourth chapter

Belonging to the second category, in truth, are all instruments strung with strings. Some are also made with keyboards, by means of which their melody is produced, such as the clavichord [*Clavichorden*], harpsichord [*Clavicymbal*],[58] symphony [*Symphoney*],[59] keyed fiddle [*Schlüsselfidel*], virginal, clavicytherium [*Claviciterium*], hurdy-gurdy [*Leim*] (I intend these as well) and all that are similar to them in their use. I will discuss these further when I write about intabulating; then I will teach you something about how you are to strive to master tablature. In order to recognise these, look below at their forms as they are illustrated.

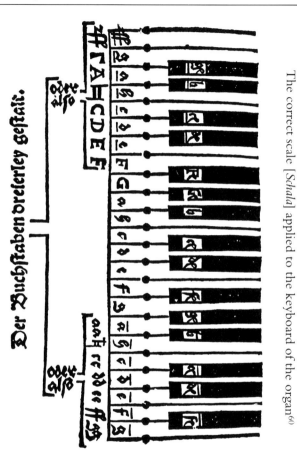

Der Buchstaben dreierley gestalt.

The correct scale [*Schala*] applied to the keyboard of the organ[60]

(*Far left:* Three forms of letters. *Left column:* Or thus. Or thus.)

Clauicordium.

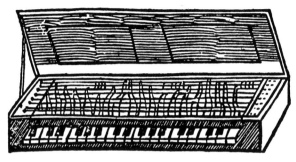

Clauicymbalum.

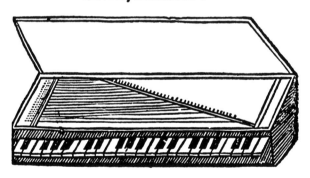

(Clavichord. Harpsichord.)

Virginal.

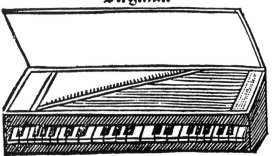

Leyer.

(Virginal. Hurdy-gurdy.)

Clauiciterium.

Schlüſſel Fidel.[61]

(Clavicytherium. Keyed fiddle.)

The second type of string instruments, which have no keys [*schlüssel*], but rather frets [*bündte*], by which they are correctly fingered and made to sound agreeably.

The second type of string instruments (take note) have no keys at all, nor keyboards [*Clavir*], just frets or otherwise certain positions [*gewisse zil*] where one has to apply correct fingerings and pick out the melody, which you may obtain by means of the frets and courses [of strings]. Examples are lutes [*Lauten*], gitterns [*Quintern*][62] and large fiddles [*gros Geigen*], as this chapter shows you.

The fifth chapter

A preface concerning the old and inconvenient tablature of the lutenists, and with it a lesson on a second, well-established one, which is derived from the correct foundation of Music.

Since I have begun and have given a lesson on wind instruments, I will not neglect to say and teach, further, a few things

about[63] lutes, dulcimers [*Hackebret*], fiddles, harps [*Harffen*] and psalteries [*Psalter*] – as much as can be allowed. Do[64] not forget about organs, xylophones [*Strofideln*] and the others that are considered similar to these. I will not explain them or teach a complete foundation for them at this time; rather, I will concentrate only on how one is to write for the above-mentioned instruments according to the correctly established tablature, derived directly from music and vocal notation. Therefore I implore you lutenists in a kindly way, not to behave like bad Christians who interpret everything in the worst way. Off to the gallows with such people!

You may well say, 'It is not possible for you to speak capably about this art, for you cannot even play the lute, yet you want to address yourself to tablature.' Yes, I admit it, and I take to heart the fact that I am still far away from actual practice. Nevertheless, I have this assurance from God: that I know a little, as one does of a nearby land. Further, I have often troubled myself with, and secretly been astonished at, how the alphabetical tablature even first came about. With this knowledge, I may also justly say how it grieves me that organists are much wiser than lutenists, with all their pretences.

For the latter (it seems to me) were quite drunk at that time when they invented their tablature. Perhaps they also had no understanding, as they did not recognise the notes or the clefs [*Claves*] placed in the margin at the beginning. They might well creep off with it [i.e., their tablature], for they have strayed far from science.

Furthermore, although it has never been acceptable to me, I have been told that their tablature was invented by a lute player blind from birth.[65] If this is true, then I shall let it stand. They certainly chose a fine master! How shall a blind man (which is unbelievable) speak of this art from proper experience who has never correctly understood Music, without which all instruments are worthless? Indeed, a seeing man who is not to be surpassed in art has enough to do. Thus, I should like to say, quite simply, if someone were to ask me about it, that the blind master forced his pupils down the wrong path and made them, with seeing eyes, blind. It is no wonder that they are ridiculed, for when one blind man leads another, both of them are considered fools. When they wish to take the right roads, they only succeed, then,

in falling together into a dark hole, because they have pulled on the same yoke. Thus they do not know where to go and have perhaps even broken their legs or become completely helpless in there; and so they are all ridiculed. Therefore, if you want to pursue this art correctly, then do not pay attention to a blind man. Hear, hear what I faithfully advise, for I have also had experience in this. If you have a desire for the abovementioned arts, then you must rush with full fervour to a most gracious maiden who is very lovely, kind and charming. No[66] one has ever pleased me as much as this dearly beloved maid. She is very kind to everyone. I consider her the loveliest one without doubt. I will point out her name to you; indeed, I have often had experience with her. You must separate off the first letter of each of the six lines given above.[67] And if you put them together into syllables, then you will not have to spell them out for very long until this fine maiden is identified, for her name is common in all lands among kings, princes and other lords. She often has to nourish many a poor lad who otherwise would have to be occupied with hard work; she often makes him into the kind of man who is praised gladly by all people, and whose purse they fill with money and goods, as[68] happened to Arion at the time when he travelled over ocean and sea, quite burdened with much money and many goods, which he had increased with his harp. Among the people in Sicily he was liked and well known. Listen to what happened to him then as he began to journey home again and associated with the sailors who had been hired in his homeland. An honourable man, he trusted them completely as his best friends. As they came to the middle of the deep sea, they began to covet his money very much. Quite audaciously, they made a quick decision to kill Arion suddenly. The good harpist realised what a bad position he was in. He gave them everything he owned just to save his life, but none of the gifts was of any help at all. 'Ha ha', they shouted many times with abandon, 'throw yourself into the water, and nothing more will happen to you. We will never bring you home.' Nevertheless, he obtained permission from them to make music and to sing a song [*Carmen*] accompanied by the harp

for his own comfort and as the valediction of a condemned man. Soon a whale[69] appeared, keeping watch. As the lovely song was finished, Arion was obliged to throw himself quickly into the water. Immediately the great fish came and took him on its back so eagerly that the water could not harm him, and he did not have to stay long in the sea. In a short time it brought Arion to the shore over many great waves. Therefore[70] this art is of such quality that at this time it is loved not only by humans but also by wild beasts, whenever it is performed. I will now write no more about this; rather, I will present the subject of intabulating, as mentioned above. There will surely be someone whom it pleases.

I say again that lutenists must have a blind instructor to transcribe music the way they do; they would certainly do better to change it. Organists have pursued the matter correctly and have begun quite skilfully. From the correct art, known as Music, their tablature comes into all lands. It is not improper (it seems to me) for them to have employed their skill in this manner.

Now, since what lutenists play [*schlan*] they must intabulate out of vocal notation, it is (in my opinion) very improper for them to introduce very many more letters than are contained in the gamut and scale [*Schala und leyter*]. I have also thought seriously that it would be very much easier to understand if they used letters of the appropriate size that are available in vocal music. Just be concerned with the differences, for the nine letters from Γ up to **G**[71] are always made large, as I understand. The next eight, from **a** to **g**,[72] are all written as small letters. The highest six[73] in the scale [*Scala*] are all doubled – believe me indeed. Another method with respect to doubled letters is followed at this time in transcribing [into tablature]: they are also made single, but with tittles [i.e., lines] over them – pay heed to this. Also, the large letters are often found small, but with tittles under them.[74] Now whoever wants to transcribe music for lutes and many other string instruments from vocal notation should observe the abovementioned differences; then he will be prepared for intabulating. He must also pay attention to the notes and not leave out the vertical lines with the flags [*die strich mit den hocken*], for they provide a correct introduction to whether the notes are to be short or long.

Now then, what need do I have of many words? I will illustrate this below, as is proper, in diagrams made up very concisely. Therefore I advise you not to give up, but to train yourselves in singing; then you will not soon become distressed.

Now if, in time, you wish to set your sights further and learn to play all kinds of string instruments, then I shall not discard your tablature, for I should be condemned as a scoundrel. Nor have I written about the masters who have practised lute playing [*Lautenschlan*] for a long time.[75] You cannot teach an old dog new tricks. I know well that they will laugh at this many times. I shall give advice only to beginners on how the foundation can be quickly understood.

This tablature, as referred to here, can be used for all instruments; it is necessary only to observe at this time what each one requires according to its method. Lutes, harps, organs and psalteries now have almost the same method, in which three or four voices are commonly notated, individually, one above the other: the treble on top, then the alto and tenor, and the bass at the very bottom – you may indeed believe me. For the organ the treble is always notated on five lines first of all, and the other voices are positioned underneath, written in letters taken from vocal notation.

For the other three, as named above, all voices are appropriately made, commonly written in letters; thus the transcription is correctly carried out. With fiddles, wind instruments, and indeed also trumpets marine [*Trumpscheit*], hurdy-gurdies and [keyed] fiddles, it is appropriate for one individual voice always to be set suitably in letters, as can be noticed immediately and very easily in the transcribed pieces below. Enough of this; no more at this time, for an experienced singer can observe well, in the following diagrams, how one acts properly in such matters. Now the scale, called a foundation, is appropriately drawn on the neck of the lute; it shows quickly at this time where *mi* and *fa* [i.e., the semitones] are on the lute.

Lauten.

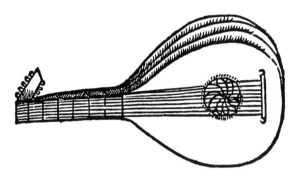

Quintern.

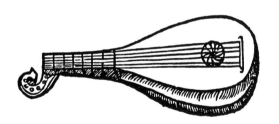

(Lute. Gittern.)

The musical scale with the old unfounded tablature, applied to the neck of the lute[76]

(*Top left:* First fret. *Bottom centre:* This open [string] is.)

Here is the correct tablature, which is taken from the correct foundation of Music, written in a proper manner by itself on the neck of the lute.[77]

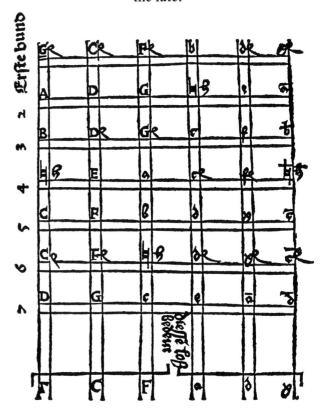

(*Top left:* First fret. *Bottom centre:* This open [string] is.)

**Here learn to finger the letters [*Claves*]
between the frets with a retuning [*ym abzuge*]
of the lute.**[78]

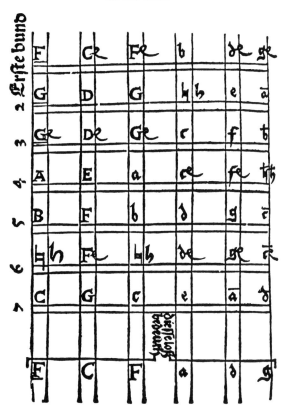

(*Top left:* First fret. *Bottom centre:* This open [string] is.)

The sixth chapter

**How music is to be transcribed from notes
into letters for lutes, harps, psalteries and
other, similar instruments, according to the
correct tablature based on Music.**

Since I have proposed here a second tablature for the lute and not reported everything that applies to it, hear further what kind of form it has. Lutenists, when they intabulate, handle it a little differently from organists and their like, although they do not deviate much from each other. Lutenists compensate themselves [for having an overly complicated tablature] and do not transcribe the treble in notes; they also do not use the five lines as organists do in their stacking up [of voices]. I say indeed that they truly transcribe all the voices from notes into letters, but in such a way that the treble always has priority on top and the others (as reported above) are placed directly under it.

Also, when they arrange three voices together, I know that lutenists now write the treble, the highest voice, solely by means of letters with stems. The other voices, notated under it, commonly have a simple form: they are written without flags. Observe, however, in these outward appearances, that a simple letter commonly has the value of the letter, having a stem, above it; and thus the simple letter is always counted the same as the letter set above it, which has a stem. If the highest letter is made with two flags [*zweyheckicht*], then the simple letters that are found directly underneath it are also executed in the same way. Yet I say to you at this time that it would be more proper and much better if it could happen by chance in the case of a simple letter found underneath one with two flags, for the simple one to be held out with the finger, functioning as a bar [*als mit eim prange*], until the course of the beat of the flagged letters above it is completed. Then you may begin another beat. You should also observe further in this connexion that the tone produced by this finger will be heard and perceived to be somewhat longer than usual. Therefore practise this method seriously, and you will be said to be learning to play the lute correctly.

Now, if you want to measure out [the notes] correctly on the lute, do not forget the differences among the letters, which are of three kinds, as reported above. Also learn, moreover, how many notes go in a whole bar [*auff ein gantzen Tact*], and act according to what was said about the organ: that each beat [*schlag*] stands by itself, separated from the others. Then set all voices, as reported, from notes into written letters.

Further, you must strive diligently to master what these diagrams teach you. This tablature serves quite appropriately for lutes, harps and psalteries; and listen when I tell you that it may also be used properly for keyboard instruments [*auff den Clavirten*].

The old tablature together with the scale applied to it, which is very useful to know for transcribing.

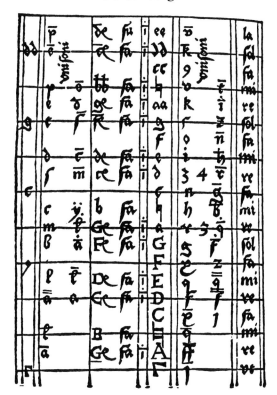

(*Across the top:* Unisons. Unisons.)

[See Appendix 9 for a table derived from this diagram of the old lute tablature.]

In the fingerings that are unplayable [*ynn den ungreifflichen griffen*] on the lute, how one letter is to be changed into another, at the octave or the unison.

It is also very necessary for anyone who wants to begin to transcribe correctly [into tablature], whether in this or another method, to see that he has learned the skill correctly. Because it often happens that there are difficult or unplayable fingerings [produced when polyphonic music is transcribed for lute], you should pay attention quite properly that you proceed correctly when you change one letter into another, which is found to be at the same pitch as the first or an octave higher or lower. This diagram will inform you how far each letter is from the other, whether it is an octave or a unison – it is more than sufficient to say this to you.

There follows a diagram showing how the letters an octave away from each other or at the same pitch can be discovered and recognised.

Concerning the letters showing octaves

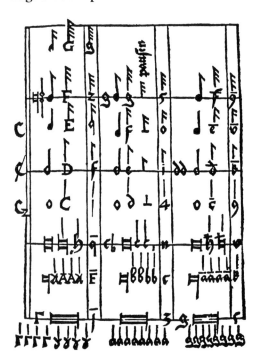

(*Top left:* Unisons. *Middle centre:* An octave away from these. *Bottom right:* Unisons.)

[See Appendix 10 for a table derived from this diagram of letters showing octaves.]

There follows a fine example of how each voice is transcribed out of notes into letters.
[See Appendices 11–14.]

How the notes of vocal notation are divided and changed into letters in the process of transcribing, and what the little strokes or flags that are placed above them mean.

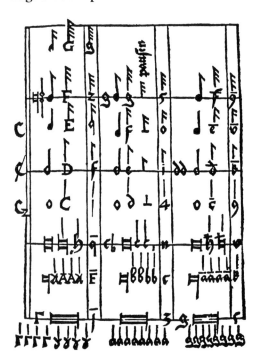

(*Top centre:* Rests.)

[See Appendix 15 for a table derived from this diagram showing how vocal notation is changed into tablature.]

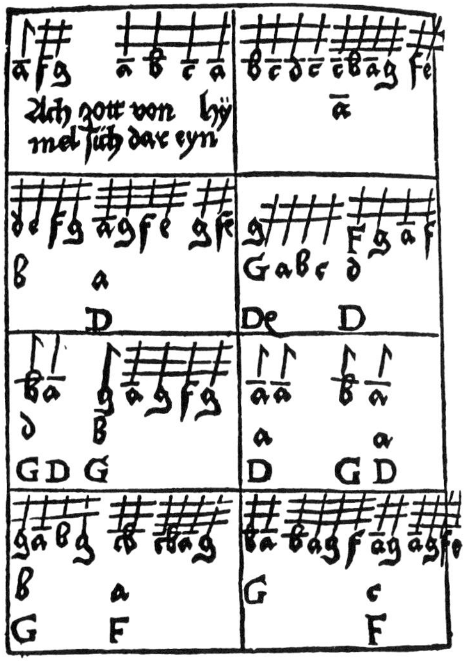
Ach gott von hÿ
mel sich dar eyn

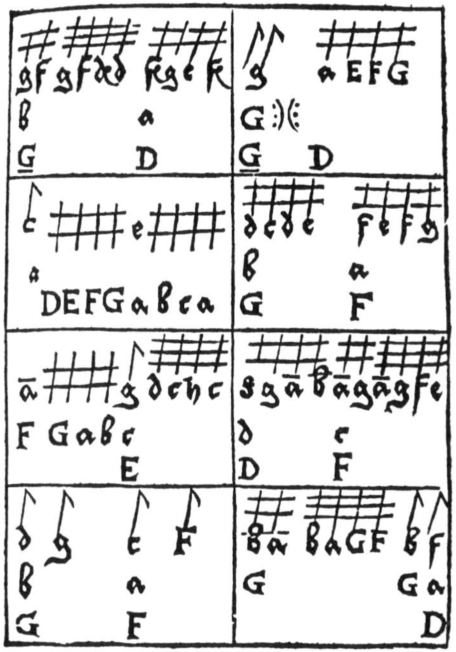

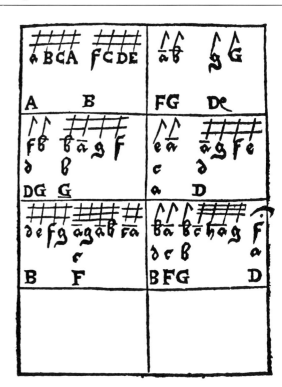

[See Appendix 16 for a transcription of this setting of 'Ach Gott, vom Himmel sieh darein'.]

The seventh chapter

Concerning the recognition and selection of good strings, which serve for instruments strung with sheep-gut strings, such as lutes, fiddles, hurdy-gurdies, psalteries, harps etc.

When you open up a bundle of strings, take the string that is as long as it has to be, correctly measured out according to the instrument. Then you should not forget the next step: stretch it between your separated hands and pluck it solely with your thumb so that the string vibrates and hums. Then notice diligently what results from this: the smaller the reaction, the better the string – I say this with knowledge. And the greater the reverberation of the string, all the worse will it be on the instrument. For a false string, I tell you plainly, can very seldom be tuned correctly.

How the selected strings are correctly allotted and strung into the six courses of the lute.

1.[80] For the **G** take a coarse, thick string. 2.[81] The **C** is suited to a somewhat smaller one. 3.[82] The **F** is even smaller and finer. Also, I say to you faithfully at this time that a moderate-sized string at the octave belongs to every course mentioned [above]. 4.[83] For the **a** provide two medium-sized strings, and join them together in the same pitch. 5.[84] Make the **d** also as just described, except that they are smaller in size. 6.[85] To the **g** belongs the very smallest, which is the purest of them all and should be completely correct with the moderate-sized strings, or else you will tune like a poor labourer. There follows a very fine diagram of this, showing how to come to agreement with it.

How the strings are first arranged on the lute, and how far the two individual strings of every course are strung apart from each other.

Tuning the strings

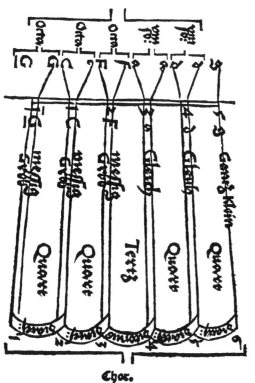

(*Far-left column:* Unison. Unison. Octave. Octave. Octave. *Left-centre column:* Very small. The same. The same. Moderate; thick. Moderate; thick. *Right-centre column:* Fourth. Fourth. Third. Fourth. Fourth. Fourth. Major third. Fourth. *Far right:* Course.)

How lutes are tuned by fourths and a third, as is now the practice.

In our time, lutenists tune lutes with the following methods. First, the string for **g** must be as high as it can stand without breaking. Tuning by fourths produces **d**[86] from **g** and **a** from **d**. A major third yields **F** from **a**. The fourth provides **C** from **F** and **G** from **C**. Thus, all of the strings are correctly set, which the second diagram artfully teaches. Observe it well, and retain it in your mind.

A second method, easier and more refined than the previous one, of tuning the strings correctly and easily, not by fourths but by octaves.

Because this kind of tuning, which makes use of fourths and a third, is very difficult, especially for a schoolboy who has not done much singing in his lifetime, I will therefore announce an easier method using octaves, which very seldom fails.

For an octave is, in truth, far easier than fourths, thirds and fifths, as a good singer must acknowledge. It is hardly necessary to say this.

Now follows the fine and easy method of tuning the lute at this time. 1.[87] Tune the string for **g** as high as you can without its breaking when you pluck it. 2. Fingered **G** [on the **F** string],[88] taken from open **g**, must be an octave lower.

3	Then	**G** an octave lower		than the		**G** [on the **F** string].
4	tune	**a** an octave lower				**ā**[89] [on the **g** string].
5	[*zeuch*]	**C** an octave lower		fingered		**c** [on the **a** string].
6	the open	**d** an octave higher				**D** [on the **C** string].

You need not worry and question any further, for all of the strings are thus correctly tuned [*gezogen*]. There follows a very fine diagram of this; be guided by it in every endeavour. A fine maiden [i.e., Music] presented this to me. My heart and soul are devoted to her. Now the diagram is likewise presented to you. My maiden will yet give me much more.

There follows a fine diagram showing how one tunes [*stymmet oder zeucht*] the strings correctly by octaves. [See Appendices 17 and 18.]

A second diagram, showing how the strings of the lute are tuned by fourths and a third. Start at the top.[90]

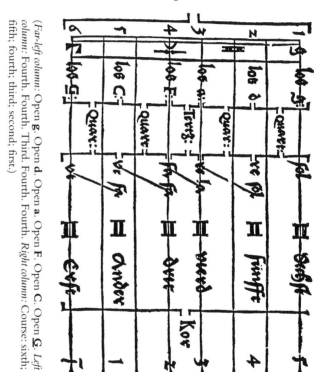

(*Far-left column:* Open **g**. Open **d**. Open **a**. Open **F**. Open **C**. Open **G**. *Left column:* Fourth. Fourth. Third. Fourth. Fourth. *Right column:* Course: sixth; fifth; fourth; third; second; first.)

Concerning three types of fiddles
[*Geigen*], and how they are strung
[*gezogen*] and correctly tuned [*gestimmet*]
together according to the correct and
true tablature.

The eighth chapter

Since I have spoken about the lute and have set down a second tablature arranged adroitly for the neck of the lute, I have reflected even further that I could apply this tablature appropriately to fiddles without causing an uproar. But it would not proceed simply, for I must receive some censure for it, although I expect it not from skilled people but from uneducated, lazy good-for-nothings who do not know what things mean. Off to the rubbish-heap with these people! Why should I waste many useless words? They will only laugh themselves to death at them.

Nevertheless, I will show, in a brotherly way, three fine types of fiddles, and how these are to be tuned simply according to the correctly established tablature, which is written on the necks and applied adroitly to the fiddles. In addition, I will not refer much to the way you should apply your fingers and the bow; rather, I will save it until later, as long as God still gives me wit. Then I will gladly and diligently share it with you and give praise and honour to God alone, without whom we can begin nothing. But His grace is also with us, and thus I will begin in His name and, with His help, introduce [the following].

How the large fiddles [*die grossen Geigen*][91] are tuned.

1. First of all, the treble[92] of the fiddle family is tuned as high as it can stand. 2. After that, tune the tenor[93] to the treble. 3. Then, immediately, [tune] the bass[94] to the tenor, as these diagrams show clearly, and as can be understood by everyone.

How the treble is first tuned by itself, separately.[95]

1[96]		$\bar{\mathbf{d}}$ [on the $\bar{\mathbf{c}}$ string]	tune	**d** string at the lower octave.
2	To the	**f** [on the **d** string]	[*zeuch*]	**F** string at the lower octave.
3	fingered	**G** [on the **F** string]	the	**g** string at the upper octave.
4		$\bar{\mathbf{a}}$ [on the **g** string]	open	**a** string at the lower octave.

Thus the treble is artfully tuned [*gezogen*]. Now see how they are all to be tuned [*zustymmen sein*] together.

How the tenor is tuned [*gezogen und gestympt*] to the treble and the bass to the tenor.

		Treble		Tenor-Alto	
1		**g**	in the	**g**	
2	To the	**d**	treble, tune	**d**	in the tenor
3	open	**a**	[*zeuch*]	**a**	at the unison.
4		**F**	the open	**F**	

5. To the fingered **c** [on the **a** string] in the treble, tune the open **C** in the tenor at the lower octave.

		Tenor-Alto		Bass	
6		**g**		**g**	
7	To	**d**	in the tenor,	**d**	in the bass
8	the	**a**	tune the open	**a**	at the unison.
9	open	**F**		**F**	
10		**C**		**C**	

11. To the fingered **G** [on the **F** string] in the tenor, tune the open **G**[97] in the bass at the lower octave.

Now you need not do any further tuning, but let them remain as referred to, for they are correctly tuned with each other. You can freely play [*streichen*] on them with the bow.

**The tablature applied to the necks of the first
type of large fiddles.**[98]

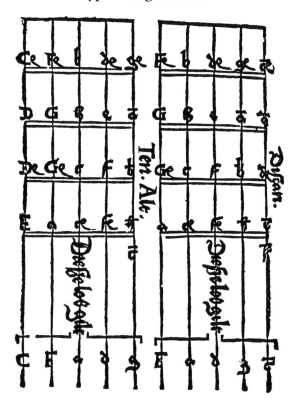

(*Across the middle:* Tenor-alto. Treble. *Across the bottom:* This
open [string] is. This open [string] is.)

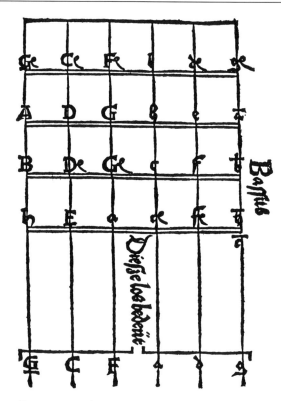

(*Bottom centre:* This open [string] is. *Middle right:* Bass.)

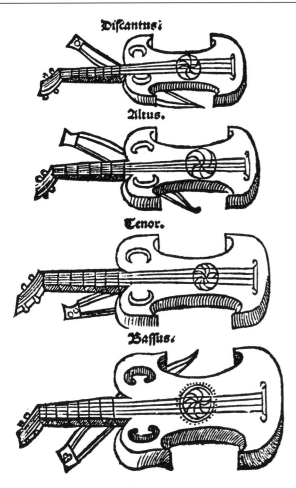

Diſcantus.

Altus.

Tenor.

Baſſus.

(Treble. Alto. Tenor. Bass.)

The second type of large or small fiddles [*grosse oder cleine Geigen*], which are found only with four strings;[99] and how they should be tuned.

The ninth chapter

Here follows a discussion of the second type of fiddles, which I have saved for now. I will teach you about it briefly, as it is my duty to do so. Tuning must be done accordingly as is shown to you in the diagrams. 1. Again, tune [*zeuch*] the treble[100] first of all. 2. The tenor[101] is to take its pitches from the treble. 3. Tune the bass[102] to the tenor as before; then I will help to praise you.

First[103] tune the highest string so high that it cannot stand one more turn [*zoch*]. Then tune [*stymme*] the others as indicated in the diagram placed below.

Concerning the tuning of the treble alone.

2
3 } To the { fingered **c̄** [on the **ā** string] / open **ā** / open **G** } tune [*zeuch*] the { open **c** at the lower octave. / fingered **a** [on the **G** string] at the lower octave.[104] / fingered **g** [on the **f** string] at the upper octave.
4

You need not tune [*stymmen*] the treble further, rather proceed as you are taught, and tune the others generally so that they agree in sound. The following diagram teaches this; proceed according to it, and you will do it right.

Concerning the tuning of these four fiddles together, see the diagram that follows.

Treble   Tenor-Alto

1
2 } To the { fingered **d̄** [on the **ā** string] / open **ā** / open **f** / open **c** } in the treble tune [*zeuch*] the { open **d** / open **a** / open **F** / open **C** } in the tenor at the { lower octave.[105] / lower octave. / lower octave. / lower octave.
3
4

Tenor-Alto   Bass

5
6 } To the { open **a** / open **F** / open **C** / fingered **G** [on the **F** string] } in the tenor tune the { open **a** / open **F** / open **C** / open **G**[106] } in the bass at the { unison. / unison. / unison. / lower octave.
7
8

Now you need not concern yourself further; rather, I tell you openly that all four of them are tuned [*gestympt*] correctly, as the fine maiden [i.e., Music] taught me.

Here, learn how the letters of tablature are to be fingered between the frets on the second type of fiddles, which are strung with four strings.

How the letters of tablature are to be fingered between the frets.[107]

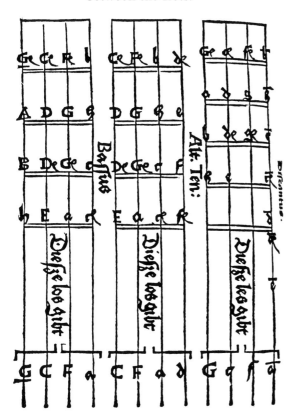

(*Across the middle:* Bass. Tenor-alto. Treble. *Across the bottom:* This open [string] produces. This open [string] produces. This open [string] produces.)

There follows the third type of small fiddles, which are strung with only three strings, tuned a fifth apart.[108]

The tenth chapter

There follows the third type of fiddles, which (I advise) you should also not avoid. They are smaller than the previous ones. Only three strings are counted on them, and they are generally found without frets. Nevertheless I say to you at this time that it is difficult to grasp [them] without frets. Therefore you should not cast them away, but practise first with frets [*auff die bündisch art*]; in this way you will become quite experienced. If, later, you cannot abide the frets, you may cut them off with a knife and fiddle away to your heart's content. Nevertheless, take note of how the strings are arranged. 1.[109] First tune [*zeuch*] the highest string of the treble [**ā**] as high as it can go without breaking immediately when you then intend to play on it and apply the bow for that purpose.

The tuning of the treble by itself.[110]

2			**d̄**[111] [on the]	tune		**d** at the lower octave.
	To the		**ā** string]	[*zeuch*]		
3	fingered		**g** [on the	the		**G** at the lower octave.
			d string]	open		

Now the treble is tuned [*gezogen*] by itself. But you must enquire still further how all four together correctly concur in their tuning [*stymmen*].

Concerning the tuning together of the four small fiddles, see the following diagrams.

1. First tune the treble by itself. 2. Then [tune] the tenor[112] quite accurately to the treble. 3. And set the bass[113] to the tenor; thus you will have very good fortune in tuning. Further, you should look diligently at what this diagram gives you.

There follows the tuning together.

Concerning the tuning together of the four small fiddles.

		Treble	in the	Tenor-Alto	in the	unison.
1		open **d**		**d**		unison.
2	To	open **G**	treble	**G**	tenor	unison.
3	the	fingered **c** [on	tune [*zeuch*]	**C**	at	lower octave.
		the **G** string]	the open		the	

		Tenor-Alto	in the	Bass	in the	unison.
4		open **G**		**G**		unison.
5	To	open **C**	tenor	**C**	bass	unison.
6	the	fingered **F** [on	tune	**E**[114]	at	lower octave.
		the **C** string]	the open		the	

Thus, each one is tuned [*gestympt*] by itself, and all four together, in the proper manner. Also, you should not be very surprised that I do not write anything in particular about how the alto is tuned [*gezogen*] to the others, for I tell you truly that the alto and the tenor are always the same. This is indicated in all of the diagrams.

There follows the scale or tablature skilfully applied to the neck of the third type of small fiddle.

The scale [applied to] the small fiddles.

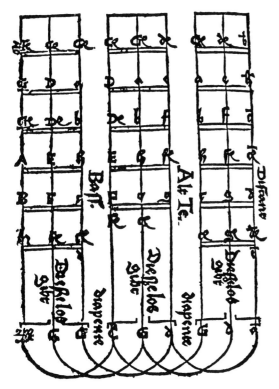

(*Across the middle:* Bass. Tenor–alto. Treble. *Across the bottom:* This open [string] produces. Fifth. This open [string] produces. Fifth. This open [string] produces.)

How to intabulate properly and correctly for all fiddles and other musical instruments on which only one voice is played.

The eleventh chapter

If you want to transcribe for fiddles or otherwise for all kinds of instruments on which one voice is played, then observe what I shall now refer to. You must not proceed as set down above concerning the organ and the lute; rather, there is a somewhat different method, which I will show you at this time. If you are not able to play from notes, then follow these instructions properly, and transcribe each voice separately out of vocal notation into appropriate letters. Thus, anyone may set down a voice for himself, as I will now show. Nevertheless, I think one is still much better advised to make use of notes.

In this way, one does not have to have the toil and trouble that are accumulated through transcribing. Whoever is intelligent can understand this. It will not be suitable for coarse clods.

Four small fiddles with frets and with three strings.[116]

Dircantus.

Altus.

(Treble. Alto.)

Tenor.

Baſſus.

(Tenor. Bass.)

There follows a tablature transcribed from notes into letters, and it serves for all monophonic instruments.

Tablature for all monophonic instruments

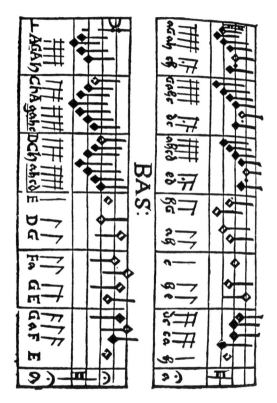

(*Across the middle:* Bass. [Tenor.])

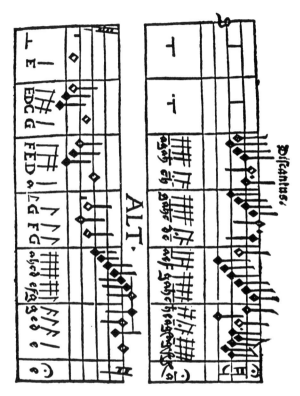

(*Across the middle:* Alto. Treble.)

[See Appendix 19 for a transcription of this tablature for monophonic instruments.]

The third type of string instruments,
which have neither keys [*schlüssel*] nor
frets, but many courses of strings, on
which one, two, three or four voices can
be produced or played.

The twelfth chapter

There follows the third type of string instruments, which
have neither frets nor places [for fingering]. They are distinguished only through courses. You should nevertheless
not avoid them. Examples are harps, dulcimers and psalteries,
which are used in our time.

Dackebreth.

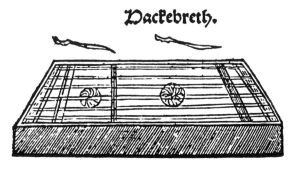

(Dulcimer.)

The tablature applied to the harp[118]

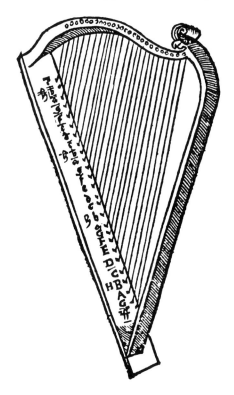

The tablature applied to the psaltery[119]

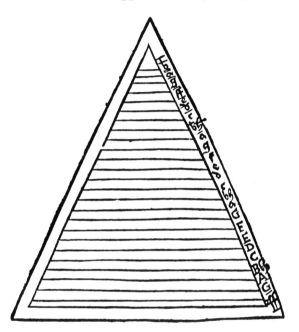

There follows the fourth type of string instruments, which also have no keys or frets, rather one, two or three courses of strings.[120]

The 13th chapter

The fourth type of string instruments, I tell you, comprises those that also have neither frets nor keyboard; rather, one generally notices them now with one, two or three courses. Examples are small fiddles,[121] and I also include the trumpet marine, which is long but nevertheless not very wide. Hear me also in this matter. Because they have no measuring-off [of places on their fingerboards], their playing method is very difficult to grasp; it is possible only through a considerable amount of practice. Nevertheless they can have frets after all, if one wants to use them to learn the tunings. When you know how to do this and cannot stand them, then cut them off with a knife, as mentioned in the discussion of the [other] small fiddles. Now see what they look like, below.

Four small fiddles without frets and with three strings[122]

Difcantus.

Altus.

(Treble. Alto.)

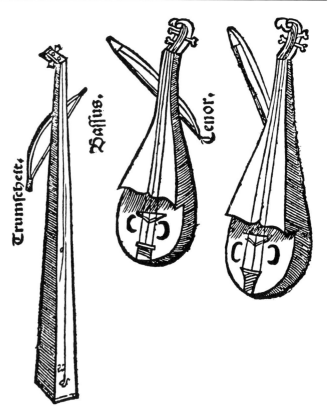

(Trumpet marine. Bass. Tenor.)

There follows the third category of musical instruments, whose sound [*Melodey*] is produced neither by pipes [*Pfeiffen*] nor by strings, but by sounding metal [*ertzt*], as follows.

The fourteenth chapter

The third category comprises all instruments that are made adroitly out of metal [*Metall*] and other substances that sound, just as a hammer sings on the anvil. Examples are small bells [*zimbeln*], xylophones [*Strofidelen*], bells [*Glocklein*] and other instruments like these.

(Anvil with hammers.)

How Pythagoras obtained several intervals – for example the octave, fifth, fourth and unison – by striking hammers on the anvil, how he weighed their proportions, and how he compared them to each other.

It will not cause much harm here, since the four hammers are illustrated below, if something more is written about what Pythagoras accomplished. He once went into a blacksmith's house, where he heard the noise of hammers. They were being struck on the anvil, and that pleased him very much indeed. 1. He had the first and fourth weighed; they proved to be an octave apart, and the first was discovered to be again as heavy as the fourth, when it was produced. 2. He then weighed the first and third hammers together very carefully. The first was one and one-half times heavier than the third, as the teachers tell us. From these the kind of sound was heard that is identified as a fifth in vocal music. 3. The first was also compared to the second, and a proportion of four to three [*sesquitertz*] was established.[123] Together, these two hammers sounded the way a fourth does when sung. 4. Further, the second was indeed compared to the third at the proportion of nine to eight [*sesquioctaff*]. Their sound was recognised as a major second, which is called a whole-tone in vocal music.

Thus, from the hammers, an octave, fifth, fourth and whole-tone were discovered at that time. I write this now not from my own experience; rather, the books written by the ancients have taught me. We must believe them, if possible. Concerning this, look at the following picture; there you will see this more clearly than in the description.

Pythagoras weighs the hammers with each other without handles and observes how much heavier one is than the other, and also what kinds of tones [*resonantz*] come from them.

Pythagoras

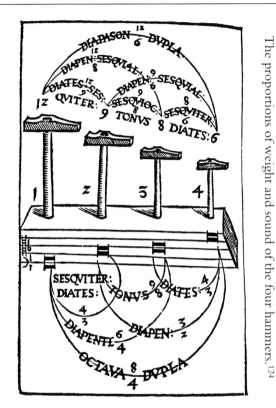

The proportions of weight and sound of the four hammers. 124

(*Top:* Octave: dupla. *Across the middle top:* Fifth: sesquialtera. Fifth: sesquialtera. *Across the lower top:* Fourth: sesquitertia. Sesquioctava: whole-tone. Sesquitertia: fourth. *Across the upper bottom:* Sesquitertia: fourth. Whole-tone. Fourth. *Across the middle bottom:* Fifth. Fifth. *Bottom:* Octave: dupla.)

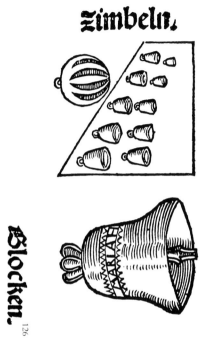

(*Top:* Small bells. *Bottom left:* Bell.)

Here is the scale or tablature applied to the xylophone.[127]

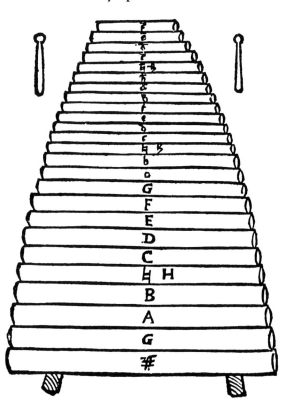

The conclusion of this book

At the beginning in the preface, I indicated briefly what propelled me the most to write this book and bring it out in print: namely, so that a short, clear method, manner and correctly formed model would be presented in the simplest way for the sake of young people and all others who are first learning to play wind instruments, fiddles, lutes, harps and other instruments, in order that they could also be instructed in instruments easily and artfully, just as they were taught to sing, easily and pleasingly, earlier in my first book about Music. For this reason, my diligent request and desire for young people and others who are first beginning to study instruments is that they will be commended to this book, receive it as a gift, and study diligently – which will without doubt increase them in noticeable usefulness and piety. In this I also wish, in a diligent and friendly manner, to have implored and exhorted all famous musicians and those practised in this art to employ all possible diligence, with a Christian attitude, to manifest this noble art openly for the use of their neighbours, so that God might be praised and lauded to eternity. Amen.

**Printed at Wittenberg
by Georg Rhau,
1529**

Instrumental Music in German
[*Musica instrumentalis deudsch*],

containing the foundation and application of the fingers and tongue to many kinds of wind instruments [*Pfeiffen*]: recorders [*Flöten*], crumhorns [*Kromphörner*], cornetts [*Zincken*], pommers [*Bomhard*], shawms [*Schalmeyen*], bagpipes [*Sackpfeiffen*], Swiss flutes [*Schweitzerpfeiffen*] etc.; also concerning the three kinds of fiddles [*Geigen*]: the Italian, the Polish, and the small hand-fiddle [*kleinen handgeiglein*]; and how their fingering patterns are also measured out skilfully on lutes [*Lauten*]; also concerning the monochord and the skilful tuning of organ pipes and small bells [*zimbeln*] etc. – comprised in brief and now newly prepared in the simplest and most understandable manner for our schoolchildren and other common singers by

Martin Agricola
in the year of Our Lord 1545.

Lady Music

To the honourable and wise lord Georg
Rhau, book printer, leader and patron of
the noble Lady Music in Wittenberg, my
most gracious, dear lord and defender, I,
Martin Sor or Agricola, wish the grace
and peace of God.

Honourable[1] and most gracious lord Georg Rhau, you know that I approached you, in the recent past, about printing several instrumental pieces or exercises for me, and I received a good response, in which your good will and counsel to serve me in this matter were indicated. Thus, I cannot hide my feelings any longer from you. The[2] first reason is that I notice many fine young boys and lads near you in Wittenberg and also in our praiseworthy school, who strive capably and become competent in the other musical practices such as plainsong and measured music (which pleases me heartily). Because of this the honourable council of Magdeburg

has earned no[3] small praise and good reputation in all lands, thanks to our school, for all students in the schools of almost all of Saxony are now fed and cared for along with schoolmasters, singers, holders of bachelor's degrees and, in cities and towns, often also with preachers. The second reason is that it seems to me that the Instrumental [Music] that I brought out 16[4] years ago[5] is too obscure and difficult to understand for boys at several places.[6] I now wish to serve them further, according to my abilities, in this noble art – namely in instrumental music, which,[7] for those who know it, expels much useless speculation, fantasy and ideas from the mind and is the source of remarkable recreation and diversion (as I have experienced); and, above all, so they can praise God, who has given this delightful and joyful art – with which the Holy Angels will also praise Him without ceasing and laud Him to eternity (as is written in the

Apocalypse)[8] – to us dejected and miserable men in this vale of tears, so that we might praise Him in many musical ways, namely with singing and playing of wind and string instruments [*mit singen, Pfeiffen, und Seitenspiel*], like the royal prophet David and also Moses, Solomon etc. For the reasons just expressed, I have considered it not only useful but also necessary to prepare a second Instrumental [Music], concerning many kinds of instruments, very clearly and in the simplest and most understandable way for our schoolchildren and others who desire it, and to have it put into print before the abovementioned pieces, which

are composed especially and with diligence in instrumental style [*nach Instrumentischer art*]. And, thereafter, if it comes to pass, I also intend to have the lessons in question printed.[9] Although, my dear lord Georg Rhau, several people who have shamefully scorned the Instrumental [Music] and me on account of it, might almost have discouraged me from my intended and useful writing, I reasoned finally that, indeed, because they speak about the subject so monastically (as in a monastery, where one lives quite meditatively and sings only plainsong without any musical instruments)[10] and perhaps do not understand anything in particular of this noble art, you[11] might therefore excuse them this time; you will not follow them, but rather Moses,[12] David and many other excellent people who have thought very highly of it (as the Psalter etc. indicates) and have presented and bequeathed us examples of how to praise God in various ways. Now in our own time, among many others, Dr Martin Luther (God be with him and grant him a long, healthy life) also does the same thing. Thus, come what may, I have nevertheless proceeded in this, my good project, useful for schoolchildren. I know well, though, that whoever renders a service to many people

cannot satisfy each one; but it should not be ceased just because of that. But, you scorner, watch out: my horse will kick back at you! I hereby send this Instrumental[13] Music to you,[14] my gracious, dear lord and particularly good friend and supporter, one who is not an insignificant collaborator in the cause of bringing to light the noble Lady[15] Music and all that belongs to her, quite clear, understandable and finely adorned. I request in the most friendly manner that you will first print it most diligently in your printing house, and then that you will let it – like both of its predecessors, also dedicated to you[16] – be commended to your protection

as my dear defender, and that you – as an excellent, strong
man, armed with this art – will help to shield and defend me,
should it become necessary, from the scorners who are now
much in evidence, although they either know nothing
themselves or do not want to be of any help in these
necessary matters. I am always willing and inclined, in return,
to serve you as my gracious, dear lord and protector, with
whom I have conversed a great deal in friendship and good
will, although not yet in my entire lifetime in person, but
nevertheless through correspondence. Thus,[17] may God be
with all of

yours and with His, among whom I am also. Given at
Magdeburg, in the house of the honourable and wise lord
Heinrich Ahlmann, with whom I have lived for a long time
and from whom much good has befallen me, for which, in a
very friendly manner, I always thank him and all others who
have done good to me. May God give him, you and us all
eternal life after this fleeting one. Amen. In the year of Our
Lord 1545, on the 14th day of April.

**Martin Agricola,
your willing disciple.**[18]

The book presented to the reader

My[19] dear reader, listen to me: I will now give you very good advice. If the gentle maiden please you (I refer to the instrumental side of Music, fine and beautifully adorned), then come, let me be commended to you.

Martinus Sore

Truly,[20] it seems to me at this time that everything printed here liberally with diagrams, as they are called, could not be written by hand by anyone. Even if one were to offer two dollars [*zwen Taler*], he would not get it (I know this for a fact); much less would a good painter paint such diagrams for that price.

Since[21] this small little book stands ready without any effort on your part, presented quite neatly and succinctly, why not buy it for so little money?

The first chapter, concerning many kinds of wind instruments, such as recorders, crumhorns, cornetts, pommers, shawms, bagpipes, transverse flutes [*queerpfeiffen*] etc., and the application of the tongue.

Preface

If you want to comprehend quickly the basis of fingering notes on the abovementioned wind instruments, my initial advice is that[22] you learn to sing properly, and then you will surely succeed in your study – believe me truly. I know this, therefore I venture to speak, not only about the wind instruments cited, but also about all instruments that are now in use on earth or are yet to be invented. When a student cannot sing, he will not gain much and will barely become established in art; rather, he will remain a dabbler.

Therefore, little boy, learn now, in your early years, to sing correctly in a musical way; let no diligence be spared. You can easily do this in schools, where art is now flourishing and is taught from morn till night. Indeed, because it goes begging,[23] it also offers itself to everyone, but few come forward to embrace it wholeheartedly and show it off joyfully. Thus, as I have observed, when something becomes too commonplace, it is scorned.

But who this noble art may be, I will show you clearly. She is properly called Lady[24] Music, well known in all lands. In the presence of emperors, kings and lords, she[25] has to nourish many poor fellows. Capable singers and trumpeters, pipers and fiddlers she protects; kettledrummers and also lutenists, organists, harpists and many like these all have to live from her favour – take note. Indeed, I say at this time that

none has ever pleased me more than this tender[26] maiden. Therefore, to me, she is the loveliest of all. And if, long[27] ago in the passion of youth, I could have had such an opportunity as boys have now, I would have employed this art differently; for nowadays there are many schoolchildren who go astray like cattle and take no interest in it. If they would just participate in it, they could seek to learn something from it and not mislead themselves. But because they scorn this art and do not consider its usefulness, they remain the coarsest clods, like crude country bumpkins, and sing the way a donkey does when it carries sacks to the mill, or the way a nightingale comports itself in singing when it torments cows.

Therefore, because they proceed in this manner, their ultimate reward is shame and ridicule, not just from other people, for they also deride themselves when they begin to grow old and experience this through understanding (as I have heard from many who thus foolishly squandered their youth), saying[28] 'Shame on me! It is a disgrace that I spent my time in such a way and learnt nothing about singing. I have led myself astray. I would now give a lot to be able to sing a little.'

'I really wanted to do my best in schools. I realise that I cannot sing; then I am ashamed because the boys have a greater understanding of it than I do. I cannot become a schoolmaster or get a bachelor's degree. I am much too inferior to be a cantor, too coarse a servant to be a deacon. They wanted to make me a sexton if only I could sing a little. I would be interested in instruments, but I know nothing of song. I often come upon good fellows who make merry with singing, piping and fiddling, and show themselves to be happy doing this. Then I am like a mute post or, among birds, the owl. I am ridiculed, and justifiably so; because of this I have to be ashamed to say to them publicly that I once went to school.'

'Oh I was foolish in my youth not to have considered the virtue of noble Music, fine and gentle. Now it is my own fault.'

O youth, youth, if you were clever, you could not receive enough gold; indeed, you could not be paid enough. Therefore, boy, reflect on this story and employ your young years well. It won't hurt you, believe me.

And generally, whenever the coarse, worthless braggarts who understand nothing about song come[29] to dinner, no one can sit ahead of them. They pay no heed to the way it [i.e., singing] should go, and one has to endure the babble [*hebdehe*] that is the best vocalising [*Coloratur*] they can produce, so their song sounds almost as bad as the voice of a donkey from behind. Yet I have indeed heard a proverb in the past that goes like this:

> He who cannot sing
> Always wants to plunge in,
> And he who knows a lot about it
> Generally refrains.

When I hear such useless howling, I immediately think to myself that they are concerned only when they talk foolishly about themselves. If you do not wish to learn good art and virtue in your youth, then henceforth remain a donkey as you began, you fool.

If you did not desire music, you are now not worthy of it. Make haste! You have waited too long. You frittered away your time in your youth.

Now[30] rich boys generally have no desire for this art, for they are always bragging about their money, as is the custom of the world, which[31] always scorns the arts and only aspires after its mammon. If it is already heaped up with the disadvantage of others, then the world will indeed end up in the Devil's cauldron.

But let this be said to you. I am not one of the oldest men, but[32] I have experienced this many times and will therefore not hold back the truth, namely that many a proud, rich man has gained a great ruin like this. He may have worn gold on his head, but he became such a poor wretch in the end that he got up, ran away with shame, and furtively fled the country; otherwise he would have had to suffer poverty, since[33] all of his property was squandered. He didn't even know enough, I say freely, to hold the job of a sexton. I shall not say what would be better. This is the way it goes when your purse is empty and you have no skill: all your cunning is lost.

Try what you will, all your stratagems are of no avail. If you lack money and have no skill, then your plans are in vain. You will surely remain a beggar. If you wanted to do heavy labour, then you might succeed somewhat, but you will not sing happily as you surely did many times when you were still a rich man.

I[34] must tell you a story – let it suit you – about a soldier who had squandered all of his money, had supported himself in foreign lands, and was obliged to travel on even further. He thought it over fully: 'What shall I do now so that I can preserve my life? My money is gone, I see no way out.' Nevertheless he reasoned very quickly: 'Shall I go begging? That is odious to me. The peasants here in the country do not give alms. The regiment does not help in this situation. Really, I must do something else so that I shall not perish here.' Suddenly he set his mind to it: 'Aha! I still know a noble art with which I will obtain favour, and[35] it is called Music.' Quickly he took his lute in his hands and[36] played in the manner of Arion, briskly and cheerfully at the same time. Then he had no further need, for he did not have to beg. In short, Music helped him out of the country in which he was entirely unknown. And[37] it happened in this year, as I was told, in fact, by a nobleman, the man called Schlywen,[38] whom many people know well.

Therefore,[39] dear Music, thanks to you for supporting many poor fellows with your sweet song and turning away hunger and trouble from them. Think on this, little boys, and let her be commended to you.

For money and possessions are quickly squandered, but honour and art remain forever valuable as long as we live on earth. Therefore,[40] rich boy, pay close attention and provide yourself in your youth with good arts and virtue, so that (as Cato teaches) you may support your poor life when your great wealth is gone and you do not have to enter the ranks of beggars.

A tetrastich by a certain poet[41]

Riches pass away, great homes pass away;
And gold, high station, clothing, things of ivory –
   they pass away.

Only the immortal glory of the muses lives:
It is not overcome by military forces or old age.

Let[42] this be a warning to you rich boys, for in truth I must speak to you because I am your teacher and daily perceive your lack of diligence. This happens right here in school, especially[43] in music, which is certainly the most prominent of all the liberal arts, as the ancients sufficiently testify. They considered as gods those who were experienced in it, as we read about Arion, Orpheus and many others. Therefore pay attention to your playing, so that in old age you will not lament the chronicle of your misspent youth.

I have been astonished to see, when boys come to Wittenberg and especially to the university, how they fare with their fellow students, who, when they sit down at the table or get up from it, joyfully engage in singing and playing instruments such as lutes, fiddles and winds; or they pick up harps and other instruments. Then these pampered children sit there like miserable wet cats, just as if they had never been present when music was taught, or otherwise when singing was practised. They well understand money in their purses, but they do not know the slightest thing about this honourable pastime. They should be called coarse blockheads.

Just as a donkey plucks the strings or is adept at playing the bagpipe, they show themselves in this way in such joyful activities. Really, it would be better if they were sent away to another place to play on horns for the coarse, worthless fellows who have wasted much good time. In our schools and elsewhere, they are coarser than bean straw. They cannot blame me for it, for I do not allow myself to be found wanting, as the boys who have studied with me must attest.

All right, then; let that be said to you in jest. Receive it, then, in good faith. Truly, I mean very well, as a faithful teacher does.

In addition I really ought to say more and[44] give a lesson to the poor, but time does not permit it. Nevertheless, hear a brief instruction.

If this pertains to the rich, you ought to study it all the more, you who have neither money nor possessions, for necessity demands this. If you don't want to pound with the hammer or thresh with the flail, carry[45] stones to the wall or load the manure cart, bespatter yourself with wet lime, slave away at the rudder or otherwise consign yourself to a ship and risk your life there, have little rest on a farm, tend donkeys or cows, dig ditches, remain a day-labourer forever, be a messenger, a common hay-cutter, a loutish fisherman or a poor, clumsy man; if you don't want to stand at the forge, wield the blacksmith's hammer and eke out a hard existence; if you don't want to chop with the carpenter's axe, work with the wedge, push the plough or remain a lump, then learn this lesson with all diligence in your youth.

Thus you will escape from this and gain honour, possessions and livelihood. An old dog cannot be taught new tricks; therefore consider this in your youth. O you parents, now pay attention and send your children to school.

But[46] do not be eager to become a papist priest. They scorn marriage and are always chasing after whores; they[47] are also the most evil blasphemers of God, as is generally observed in all of them. It is a disgrace among Christians that there is suffering in this land because they do not want to become converted, but rather fight tooth and nail to keep God's word indeed from prevailing. Therefore we say justly, 'Woe, woe to them.'

But take care, you priestly rogue: the Devil will torment your belly when you do not turn to God but instead blaspheme and scorn Him with your papist conduct such as ringing [bells] or reading the Mass. It[48] is well known that your sacrament is only a simple element, namely bread and wine and nothing more, as is proved in many existing teachings of holy scripture by honourable men and God's heroes

such[49] as Luther, who will prove it, and also by my gracious lord, a well-known licentiate called Nicolaus[50] Glossenus.[51] And many more besides them will bear witness to this. Why do you boast so much, you papist? For all your piety, you are a blasphemer of God. Crawl away and hide; it's about time!

Is it your intention, then, to blind our eyes? As a conjuror in his booth does with Old Nick, moving him now up, now down, so you carry on a ceremony with your wafer as you stand like a fool before the altar and have nothing there but bread and, likewise, simple wine. Still you consider it a great miracle. You often stick the wafer into the monstrance or shut it up completely in the wall when you are not running about revelling and parading here and there through the streets. Nowhere is it written that you are to go about with conjurors or shut [the wafer] up in a closet; rather, you should employ it as Christ has commanded you – I say this to you frankly.

For[52] he says, in this case, 'Take, eat and drink ye all of it.' I think this certainly would be clear enough if you, poor man, were clever. It[53] is a mystery that you take only bread with you and not wine. When[54] you get hot in the procession and break out in a sweat because of the heat, don't you also get thirsty, you fat priest, you who comport yourself like an ape? But away with you, you useless fool, for the peasants observe truly that you associate with conjurors, blasphemers of God, and nothing but false show. Even the children in the street understand it suitably. Therefore clear out, you useless papist, along with your pope, the Antichrist. Because he will not be converted, God will overthrow the Villain, namely Paul III,[55] who has never been pious, but rather, up to now, in his way a deceiver of Christians. May Beelzebub befoul his grey beard,[56] for he still continually incites the Emperor[57] to sharpen his sword in order to annihilate the Christians completely. May God give the Emperor many good years and illuminate him with His word,

and protect him from such murder, and also graciously save him from the evil priests and monks and from all other papists, who daily move back and forth about him.

And may God give the Pope the agony of hell. He will surely be there eternally with all of his followers and comrades who do not want to do penance. May this come to pass in honour of God's name; we all say 'Amen' to that. Now you have been told, Paul. I cannot curse you forever, but just once more: may God smite you quickly and keep us in His word.

For other strong, powerful imprecations you may look in the book written by Dr Martin [Luther], completed[58] in the forty-fifth year, entitled Against the Papacy in Rome, Founded by the Devil,[59] in which he presents his estimation of your villainous nature and casts you, along with your comrades, into the abyss of hell. There, in eternal agony, you will all be comrades of your Lucifer.

And I may be permitted to say, indeed, as a stupid servant, that if the papists do not grasp in the book the lesson on their error, then they are quite incapable of being advised about their damnable deeds. Even if Moses were to come again, take[60] his rod in his hand, and perform miracles as he did indeed in the presence of Pharaoh, it would all be truly in vain, for they are surely hardened by God, as He did to Pharaoh.

Therefore let us observe these rhymes with diligence in such matters.

We[61] may well now guard ourselves against priests, along with their followers, such as Jews and Turks in truth, for they want to exterminate Christianity completely.

Surely[62] God has commanded the worldly powers to exterminate such blasphemers. 'Yes', a few people say, 'this is true. But who indeed can accomplish it? One must endure them in order to avoid war and strife.'

I ask you, which is of greater consequence: to anger men or God? Would it not be better to risk a conflict rather[63] than God's wrath and other affliction? If you prevent such blasphemy, God will surely ease the battle, as He certainly did before, which anyone can observe.

Indeed, if you obstruct all devils,

to say nothing of men in this case, nothing will then be wanting. You will surely come away peacefully, as has often happened in the Old Testament – observe this. But if you will tolerate the blasphemers and[64] see through your fingers [i.e., look the other way] or otherwise take gifts of which you should justly be ashamed, then you will surely feel the punishment at the end. You may refresh yourself with that.

At the same time I have not disdained anyone. If each man considers God's word and behaves so that he can stand steadfast, then he acts like a Christian.

Therefore, boy, you ought to study so[65] that knowledge and virtue may adorn you, and so that you will let yourself be employed in a correct, honourable manner in the chancellery, in the city hall, where exceedingly learned people work, in the court of law nearby, in the school (observe this very well), and in other places, as I say, of which I do not wish to write at this time.

Plato

Blessed is the state where philosophers rule, or where those who rule think like philosophers.[66]

It is not possible, I say openly,

for a good administration to endure – or for government to succeed in cities, towns and lands, or where anything of importance is present – without educated people.

Therefore[67] one well-educated man is worth more than a thousand others who are not educated. One observes this every day indeed. That is enough of this for now. I ask you not to take offence at me, for I write without any malice, solely to entice boys to the arts and the gifts of God.

Now[68] then, so that I do not make this too long, we want to get to the heart of the matter and describe in a short time how it is therefore useful.

Practice

If you want to acquaint yourself with art, then pick up the wind instrument [*Pfeiff*] in your hands with the right one on top and the left one on the bottom.[69] Thus you have found the way to begin. In addition, it will be necessary for the lowest hole on the right side on recorders [*Flöten*] to remain unfingered and to be plugged up with wax. Thus each individual hand has four holes on the common wind instrument, as the illustrated recorder indicates by means of numbers placed on it, which identify the fingers of both hands on the right side. The fingerholes are recognised by means of the numbers at the left.[70]

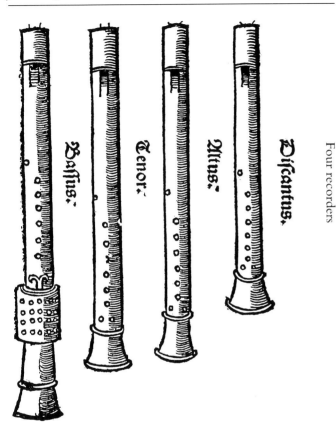

Four recorders

(Bass. Tenor. Alto. Treble.)

Identification of the numbers on wind instruments

This number {indicates that}

⊕	half of the eighth
8	the entire eighth
7	the seventh
6	the sixth
5	the fifth
4	the fourth
3	the third
2	the second
1	the first

hole of the instrument is opened.

● all holes closed; this means all opened ○.

The form of recorders

Here, you tender young boy, look at the shape of recorders and also their method.

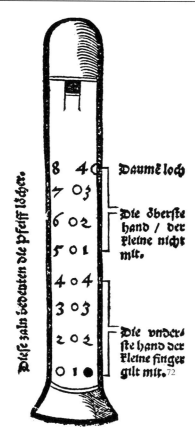

(*Left:* These numbers indicate the fingerholes. *Right column:* The thumbhole. The upper hand, not including the little finger. The lower hand, including the little finger.)

Further, you should observe diligently how things stand in these matters, namely in the other diagrams, where you will notice several numbers and other symbols next to them; you should indeed observe them also.

I will explain the first chart and then very easily demonstrate the others. This[73] circle ●, I now tell you, indicates all holes closed. It produces **G** in the treble [*Discant*], as the latter's scale [*Scala*] instructs. The numbers contained therein refer to the eight holes, which are opened as the instrument is played [*gepfiffen*], as is properly described here.

Observe this

1 signifies **a**, 2 is **b**♭ and 12 is **b**♮. Understand 13 as **c**, 1234 as **d**, 12345 as **e** and 12346[74] as **f**. 13457[75] indicates **g**, and ○[76] is all holes opened. This fingering is also made thus: 1345678, which shows **aa**. 178 is favourable towards **bb**♭.

$12 produces **bb**♮, and indeed $13 is **cc**. $1234 brings **dd**, $12345 is **ee**, $123 is **ee**♭ and $123456 is **ff**.

Thus you can easily understand the two diagrams that follow, if at all times you understand what the clef [*Clavis*; i.e., the letter-name of the note] is, and the scale. If not, then go and learn it better; you will find this in music.

On this subject there now follow three skilfully prepared diagrams, in which the illustrations are as clear as my descriptions above: first the treble of the wind instrument, and then immediately the tenor and the bass.[77] The tenor and the alto have the same method; learn this from me at this time.

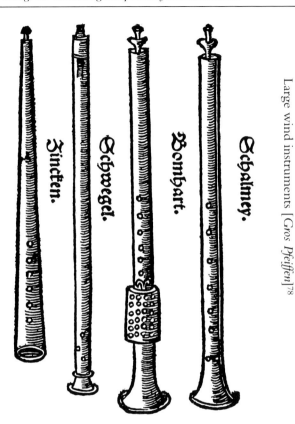

Large wind instruments [*Gros Pfeiffen*][78]

([Straight] cornett. Three-hole pipe. Pommer. Shawm.)

Precaution

Know also, my dear boys, that if you wish to have wind instruments tuned to each other, you should buy them for yourselves in fine cases [i.e., as a set], for the others are generally false.

Concerning the treble

If you want to finger the holes correctly on recorders and other wind instruments, then you should follow it [i.e., the treble] as the three diagrams indicate, for the numbers illustrated here show the patterns found on all of these. First, the way to finger the treble is recognised in this diagram.

In addition

Understand the chromatic notes [*Semitona*] – such as **c#**, **d#**, **f#** and the like – through the numbers placed here in the margin. Although[79] they decorate music elegantly, they are nevertheless seldom employed, and then only in syncopations [*Syncopirn*; i.e., cadences]. Therefore, first learn simple playing in the diatonic category [*nach dem Diatonischen geschlecht*], as the scale placed here shows. Later, this will be regarded as very easy.

An example

d̄ℓ		ee ♭		
c̄ℓ		dd ♭		
fℓ	signifies	g ♭	and the same is true
dℓ		e ♭	of the octaves.
cℓ		d ♭		

There follow the foundation and scale of the treble.

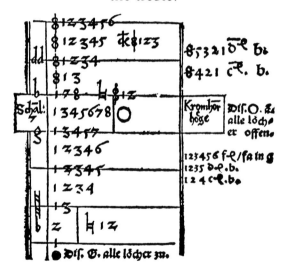

(*Across the middle:* Shawm. The top limit of the crumhorn. Treble ○, **ā**, all holes open. *Bottom:* Treble **G**, all holes closed.)

[See Appendix 20 for a composite transcription of the fingering charts for recorders and related instruments on fols. 20, 21 and 22.]

(*Top right:* [The fingering for] treble **dd**.)

Worthy of note

Crumhorns go no higher than an octave and a whole-tone [*ein Tonum Diapason*]; for example, the treble goes up to **aa**, the tenor to **d** (observe this here), and the bass reaches **G**, as indicated by the open circle. The practice of the shawms and the pommer is also announced to you here. Thus a piece designed to go higher is not suitable for these wind instruments.

Concerning the tenor and alto

I will teach well here, in the following diagram, how the tenor is fingered, and the alto also – observe this at the same time.

The foundation and scale of the tenor and alto

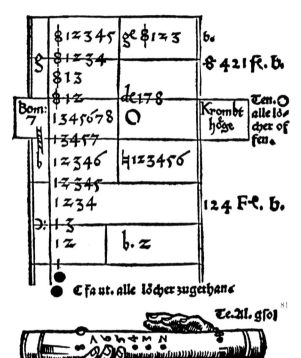

(*Across the upper middle:* Pommer. The top limit of the crumhorn. Tenor ○, all holes open. *Lower centre:* **C**, all holes closed. *Bottom right:* [The fingering for] tenor-alto **g**.)

An example of the uncommon semitones

f𝐞
G𝐞   signifies
F𝐞

g♭
a♭
G♭

Concerning the bass

You should finger the largest wind instrument, called the bass, in the manner shown here in the diagram, which is based on music.

The foundation and scale of the bass

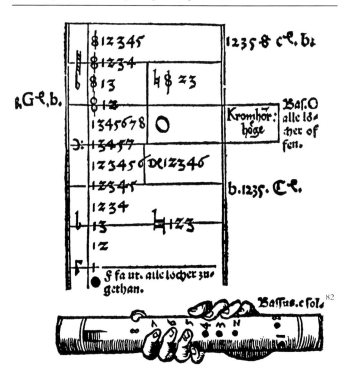

(*Across the upper middle:* The top limit of the crumhorn. Bass ○, all holes open. *Lower centre:* **F**, all holes closed. *Bottom right:* [The fingering for] bass **c**.)

An example of the semitones

c𝐞
G𝐞   signifies
C𝐞

d♭
a♭
D♭

with the same being true of the octaves.

A fine foundation, to be learnt on a small recorder [*auff einem kleinen Flötlein*] that has no more than four holes, except that when the lowest end of the instrument is also employed (as commonly happens), it may be reckoned as having five or six holes.

Further, I do not wish to omit, but rather to broach the subject of the practice of the small recorder and how the holes are to be fingered correctly and cleverly. First pick up the instrument in the right hand, or in the left without any disgrace. Your other hand will be free and independent, except that you control the bottom hole [i.e., the open end of the instrument] solely with the finger next to the thumb [i.e., the index finger], as shown in the diagram.

In this diagram, the bottom end of the instrument is also reckoned as a hole or note when it is half-fingered, as follows.

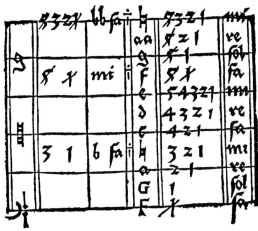

[See Appendix 5 for a transcription of this fingering chart for the small recorder with four holes.]

𝕶lein ℨlőtlein mit vier löchern. [85]

Vier Kromphörner/oder Pfeiffen. [86]

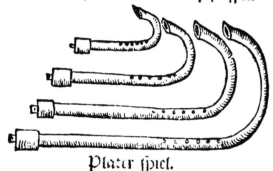

Plater spiel.

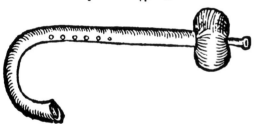

Krumphorn.

(Small recorder with four holes. Four crumhorns. Bladder-pipe. Curved horn.)

There follows another fine musical foundation showing how the notes [*Claves*] are to be fingered correctly on transverse flutes [*queerpfeiffen*].

I have described the foundation of six kinds of wind instruments as mentioned – cornetts, crumhorns, recorders, pommers, bagpipes and shawms[87] – all of which are practically identical in their fingerings.

Now I will proceed further with the foundation of the transverse flutes and bring to light distinctly as much as I can at this time. First, take this lesson from me: they have no more than six holes, as one observes, and therefore other fingerings apply to them. I tell you openly that the left hand controls three holes, and so does the right. Three fingers are to be considered here, with the little finger and the thumb left out.

How the blowing is to be effected is written in the diagrams that follow directly hereunder. The numbers have the form given in the explanation of recorders, and therefore the instruction is sufficient, for it is easily understood by anyone who is thoroughly acquainted with the preceding. Therefore, I think that not many words are necessary. Proceed according to the method given above.

The form of the Swiss flutes [*Schweytzer Pfeiffen*]

Here you see the method and appearance of these instruments correctly depicted.[88]

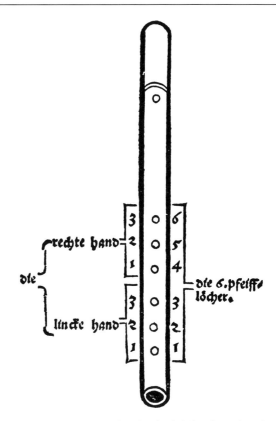

(*Left column:* The right hand. The left hand. *Right:* The 6 fingerholes.)

Four Swiss flutes[90]

𝕭𝖆𝖘𝖘𝖚𝖘. 𝕿𝖊𝖓𝖔𝖗. 𝕬𝖑𝖙𝖚𝖘. 𝕯𝖎𝖘𝖈𝖆𝖓𝖙𝖚𝖘.

(Bass. Tenor. Alto. Treble.)

A few precautions

Also, in playing, it is desirable if you blow with quivering breath [*mit zitternden wind*], for it will be observed here, just as it will be taught below in the method of the Polish fiddle,[91] that the quivering decorates the melody. It would be an important ornament [*ein gros ornat*] on organs, although it has seldom been employed up to now in German lands.[92] I hope the time has already come when organ makers do not hide and hold it back behind bushes. Indeed,[93] they might pay attention to acting properly in these matters. God has surely therefore not given this to us for us to keep it to ourselves, but rather to share with our neighbours. Everyone can strive to obtain that goal who wants to behave correctly according to God's word and does not wish to be a servant of the Devil.

Concerning the treble

You treble player, now be present. If you wish to play freely in the Swiss manner, you will find it very clearly and distinctly presented in the following diagram.

The scale and foundation of the treble

There follow three irregular scales for these flutes, transposed to the upper fourth.

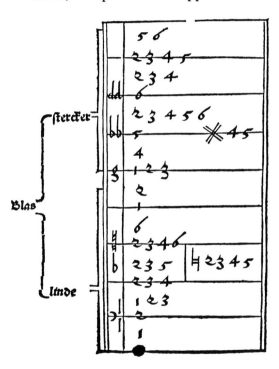

(Left column: Blow: more strongly; gently.)

[See Appendix 21 for a composite transcription of the fingering charts for Swiss flutes on fols. 26ᵛ, 27ᵛ, 28, 30ᵛ, 31 and 31ᵛ.]

Concerning the tenor and alto

If you want to learn the tenor and alto, then get yourself here right away to this fine diagram; here you will find how it should be done.

The foundation and scale of the tenor and alto

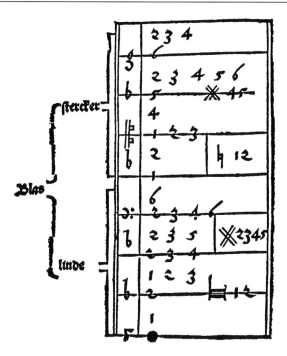

(*Left column:* Blow: more strongly; gently.)

Concerning the bass

If you want to be a proper bassist [*Bassant*] on the above-mentioned instruments, then come and pay attention indeed to what is presented to you here.

The foundation and scale [*leyter*] of the bass

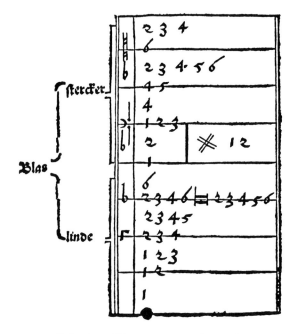

(*Left column:* Blow: more strongly; gently.)

There follows a discussion of large wind instruments, such as the trombone [*Busaun*], military trumpet [*Felttrommet*], clareta and tower trumpet [*Türmerhorn*].[94]

Some instruments, however, have no holes – just one at the top and one at the bottom, through which the melody is produced solely and completely by blowing and drawing [a slide]. Examples are the trombone, trumpets and clareta,[95] as shown here in the following illustration. I shall not say much about them at this time, for I do not yet possess the proper fundamentals; but when I obtain them, you will receive them correctly from me.[96] Nevertheless, in order not to let this merely pass, I will show pictures of them to you.[97]

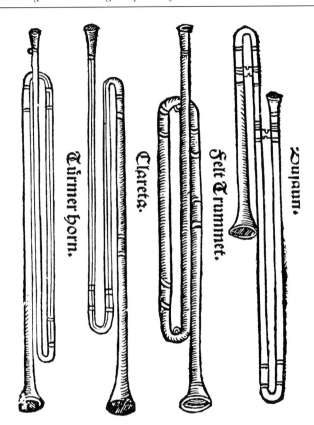

(Tower trumpet. Clareta. Military trumpet. Trombone.)

There follows yet another better and
common method of blowing and
fingering the notes [*Claves*] in a musical
manner on these wind instruments.

Further, I do not wish to keep silent, but to show another
method of the aforementioned foundation for the Swiss flutes
referred to here, which is considered the commonest and
easiest. Thus, I have also introduced it here. But do not feel
sorry that I now speak of two methods, while[98] formerly in
the German Instrumental [Music] I spoke of a third, for one
can transpose[99] the scales [*Scalas*] here just as in singing
(observe this) or as is done on organs, lutes and others in
addition, as I shall tell you. Therefore let your distrust be
gone! Thus I have presented both of them; pick the one that
pleases you. Nevertheless[100] I will speak in general: to me this
one seems the most appropriate.

How you are to understand it I will show in diagrams and let
it come forth. You can pay attention to it.

There follow the three diagrams

**There follow three other, regular scales for
these flutes.**

The scale of the treble

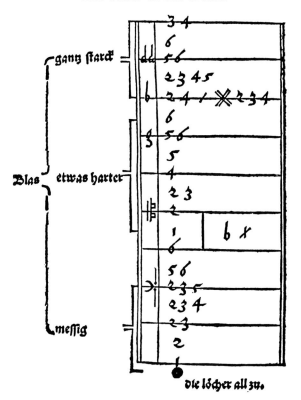

(*Left column:* Blow: very strongly; somewhat harder; moderately. *Bottom:* All of the holes closed.)

[See Appendix 21 for a composite transcription of the fingering charts for Swiss flutes on fols. 26ᵛ, 27ᵛ, 28, 30ᵛ, 31 and 31ᵛ.]

The foundation of the tenor and alto

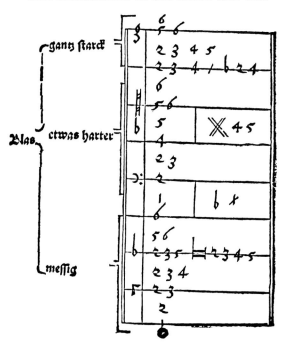

(*Left column:* Blow: very strongly; somewhat harder; moderately.)

The scale of the bass

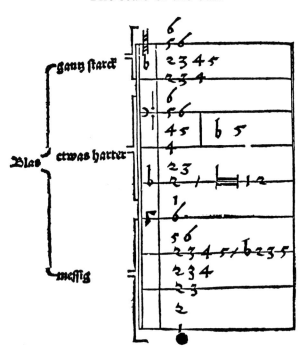

(*Left column:* Blow: very strongly; somewhat harder; moderately.)

There follows: concerning the movement or the application of the tongue to wind instruments.

There is one more thing that I will not conceal from you, which is not insignificant in wind instruments but is indeed the chief aspect – believe this for a fact. It is namely how the tongue, guided in the mouth, is applied to the notes [*Noten*].

Thus I say to you at this time that when you bring the wind instrument to your mouth and wish to play from vocal notation, then notice if the notes are long; that is, if they are maximas, longs, or just breves, out of which semibreves are commonly made – observe this.

As I understand, semibreves, minims and semiminims have the same application, and you should understand this thus: you must move your tongue and set it in motion in your mouth for each individual note, as the following example shows. The fingers and the tongue are to be coordinated, and thus the rapid passage [*Colorathur*] will sound clean; for when the tongue is set in motion before the fingers are moved from their holes, the sound is never as good as when they are both activated at the same time.

The other two fast notes, the[101] fusa and the semifusa, also both have one method of application (observe this diligently), but not in the same manner as was taught for the other notes – although some people, in their playing, produce semiminims in the way described below. You will soon observe this clearly in a very fine example. Apply your tongue accordingly to every note with artfulness, as indicated below. On bagpipes the tongue cannot be used; there it is the fingers that have control.[102]

(Bagpipe.)

Finally, I shall earn very little gratitude indeed from some wind players for this merry tale, but I don't care a whit about it. They say I make art too common; my answer is, 'I have it free from God.' It is said, 'Freely you have received, freely give it to your neighbour.'[103] You should seek not your own things, rather[104] those of your neighbour at all times.

Also, if anyone wishes to scorn me, he can very well try to do things better than I; otherwise, his cause will be false indeed. A thing can be scorned quickly, but it takes a long time to make it better. If you can show yourself to be better [than I], then I will praise you myself; if not, then keep your slanderous mouth shut and act according to God's will. All right then, enough of this for now. We want to begin the example, in which what we taught above will be proved.

There follows the example of the application of the tongue.

If you want your playing to stand the test, then learn[105] well your *di ri di ri de*,[106] for this belongs to the small notes. Thus do not let yourself be made a mockery.

Also, if you want to investigate further and learn to play divisions [*lernen colorirn*] cleanly with embellishments [*mit mordanten*] of correct proportions, you may learn this from a teacher, for it is not appropriate here for me to give instruction in this.

Example of the application of the tongue[107]

(*End of second stave:* Or thus. *Middle:* And this last one is considered the best by certain people.)

**Some people employ this method in playing
divisions and call it the flutter-tongue
[*flitterzunge*], as follows.**

Example[108]

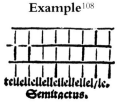

(*Bottom:* Half-bar.)

The second chapter, concerning three kinds of fiddles [*Geigen*]: the Italian, the Polish and the little one with three strings.

If you desire to study further the proper application of the bow on the fiddles that are called the Italian type, then pay attention to me at this time. Hold the bow in your right hand, and give the strokes [*gib den zügen*] the following form: let[109] them travel, always one after the other, on the strings. Employ the five notes (now observe this) – semibreves and minims, semiminims, fusas and also semifusas – in this manner: bow [*zeuch*] each one separately as it is found in the notation [*in dem gesange*]. Employ the bow appropriately so that each note has its own stroke [*zug*]. Divide the other notes – namely the maxima, breve and similarly the long –

into semibreves. Thus you will also give them their value, and this is what should happen with the [bow] strokes. However,[110] when you find a breve in the notation, you may indeed bow it with one long stroke, as the whole bar [*der ganze Tact*] requires. Let this be said about bowing. Also, the bow should have its path on the strings close to the bridge where the strings lie completely open; this will give a proper sound.

The positioning of the fingers on the neck at the very top is clearly shown in the diagrams not very far below. The numbers of the fingers are given for you on the right sides of the diagrams.

After that, move on quickly to the strings. Make the fingerings agree with the tunings [*den zügen vergleich*]; namely, as fast as you set a tuning, so quickly must you grasp the top of the neck with the fingers of your left hand, as mentioned above. Now if you cannot sing at all, well then, you will have to strive to transcribe the notes, each[111] one – where it is found – into its letter [*buchstab*], which is perceived at the beginning of the clef [*des Schlüssels*]. This comes about easily when one knows the differences among the letters,

namely, whether they should be large or small or doubled, as the scale instructs well. Observe this and commit it to your memory.

Concerning three different kinds of musical letters [*schlüssel*], which are very useful to know when transcribing music for fiddles, lutes, harps and organs.

The doubled ones thus:[112]

The small ones thus:

The large ones thus:[113]

My opinion

I consider no instrument to be as similar in sound [*melodey*] to the human voice as the fiddle. Sing into it, and you will hear yourself. That's enough chatter about this. Let us freely take the foundation presented here, contained in the three diagrams, and see how we should proceed with the practice in these matters.

There follow three artful diagrams in which the correct foundation for the large Italian fiddles[114] is contained in a very masterly way.

Concerning the treble [*Discant*]

This diagram will show you how to play the treble.[115]

Another tuning for the treble

Since one observes that the treble in vocal music seldom reaches [down to] **G**, but goes up to **dd** and **ee**, one could tune it as given here.[116]

(*Right column:* Open string: 4th, 3rd; 2nd; first. *Bottom:* Fret.)

High fiddle [*Testudo acuta*][117]

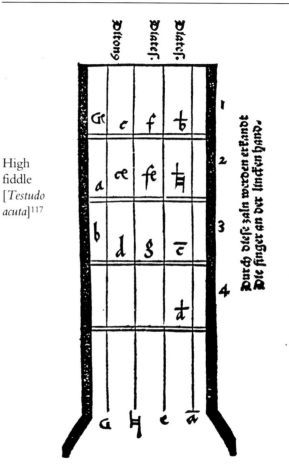

(*Across the top:* Major third. Fourth. Fourth. *Right:* The fingers of the left hand are identified by these numbers.)

97

Supplement

I think that the tuning [*zug*] given here indeed requires yet a fifth string, tuned to **dd**. This is indeed suitable for a piece that goes up to **ee** and **ff**, which is otherwise difficult to play. To be sure, it is left up to everyone to do as he pleases.

Concerning the tenor-and-alto

From this diagram you can learn quickly how the tenor-and-alto is played [*gegeigt*].[118]

Middle fiddle [*Cithara media*][119]

(*Right:* Fingers.)

Concerning the bass

This following foundation belongs to the fiddle called the bass.[120]

Low fiddle [*Testudo gravis*]

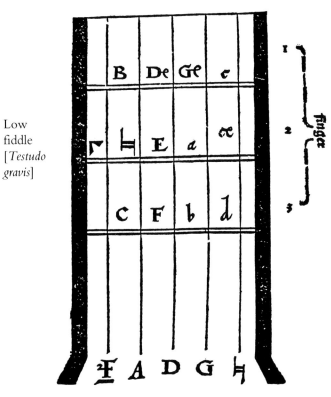

(*Right:* Fingers.)

Although one tunes the bass differently, nevertheless this seems the most suitable method. In it the fingerings are placed close together, which is not unpleasing to a fiddler [*eim Geiger*].

There follows a diagram of the other tuning.[121]

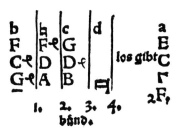

(*Right:* [Each] open [string] produces. *Bottom:* Fret.)

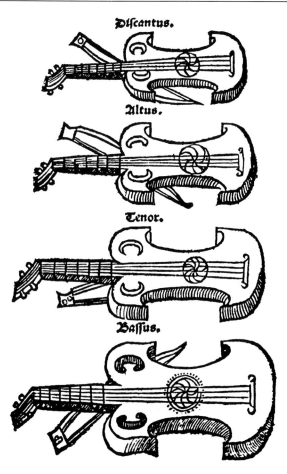

(Treble. Alto. Tenor. Bass.)

There follows: how the frets are measured off on the neck of the large Italian fiddle using the dividers [*zirckel*] according to the method of the monochord.

Finally you must observe with diligence that the frets of the fiddle are not set on the neck just for show, as is the practice of many people who take the frets off altogether and do not notice whether it sounds right when one sets his fingers down and ruins the good melody.

But there is another science, which I will communicate to you freely, involving[123] the dividers, which are the master of this science. Practise this skill. The dividers will not deceive you, for they truly cannot lie (I say) when they are properly used, as can be perceived below in the diagrams.

If you want to measure off frets correctly, you must not forget this: begin the measurement adroitly at the very top of the neck, right where the strings emanate from the little piece of wood [i.e., the nut] placed underneath, and let it go down to where you find the trestle [*Treger*] standing, which is called the bridge [*Steffen*]. There you will encounter the partition; and notice that the measurement goes no further since that is where the string is parted by the bridge. Also, if you divide up the highest string [*Quintseit*] by itself, then all will be in agreement.

You[124] may mark the beginning right away with an **ā** in the treble. Take a **d** in the tenor. Mark the bass with the letter **a**, and the end, right at the bridge, with[125] the number **0**, called zero.

Indicate with dots the places where the letters are found. When they are all measured out, stretch the frets over the neck at the points where the letters stand. Thus you will have the correct fingering positions, which are indeed distinctly and clearly included in these diagrams.

The first diagram, concerning the dividing up of the treble.

In this diagram, the way to measure off the treble is shown.

First — ā — 0 — 9 — The first part gives b♮.

Second — ā — 0 — 4 — The first part gives d.

Third — d̄ — 0 — 8 — The dividers [set at one-eighth of the distance from d̄ to 0] moved backwards from the first point give c̄.

Fourth — c̄[-] — 0 — 8 — The dividers [set at one-eighth of the distance from c̄ to 0] moved backwards [from the first point] give b♭.

divide the distance from ... up to ... into parts.

[See Appendix 22 for a table of intervals derived from the instructions for measuring off the necks of the large Italian fiddle, the Polish fiddle and the small three-string, unfretted fiddle, found on fols. 41, 41ᵛ, 42 and 49ᵛ.]

The third diagram, concerning the bass.

Here you will find the correct measurements for dividing off the bass.

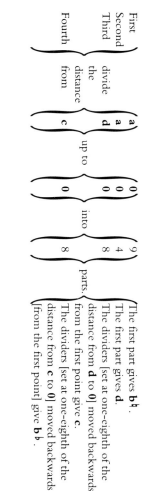

First, Second — a, a — divide the distance from — 0, 0 — up to — 9, 4 — into — parts.
Third, Fourth — d, c — 0, 0 — 8, 8

The first part gives **b♮**.
The first part gives **d**.
The dividers [set at one-eighth of the distance from **d** to **0**] moved backwards from the first point give **c**.
The dividers [set at one-eighth of the distance from **c** to **0**] moved backwards [from the first point] give **b♭**.

The second diagram, concerning the tenor-and-alto.

Here the way to measure off the tenor-and-alto is artfully revealed.

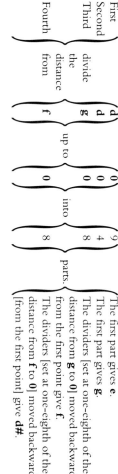

First, Second — d, d — divide the distance from — 0, 0 — up to — 9, 4 — into — parts.
Third, Fourth — g, f — 0, 0 — 8, 8

The first part gives **e**.
The first part gives **g**.
The dividers [set at one-eighth of the distance from **g** to **0**] moved backwards from the first point give **f**.
The dividers [set at one-eighth of the distance from **f** to **0**] moved backwards [from the first point] give **d#**.

There follows the method for the Polish fiddle[126] and the small hand-fiddle [*handgeiglein*].

Further, I will point out to you the second category of fiddles, which are common in Poland, on which the strings are tuned in fifths and are fingered in a different manner from the one taught above. They are stopped with the nails, and therefore the strings stand far apart from each other. In my opinion they sound quite pure and are much more refined, artful and lovely in resonance than the Italian ones. Anyone may recognise by himself what I mean by 'refined', and whether a string that is stopped with the nails does not sound brighter than one stopped with the soft fingers[127] or something else that gives the same effect. For what is soft dampens the sound, and what is hard makes the music clearer. One also produces vibrato freely [*Auch schafft man mit dem zittern frey*] to make the melody sound sweeter than it will be on the others.

Listen further to what I tell you. Because they are made without frets, it is considered somewhat more difficult to apply the fingers to them and to move the fingers between the strings. But[128] there is nothing on earth so difficult that it cannot be attained through diligence.

I will tell you how to apply your fingers to the neck through the following clear, very evident diagrams.[129]

There follows a lesson on how the abovementioned fiddles[130] are tuned together correctly, and first how the treble is tuned separately, all by itself.

First tune the highest string [**a**] to as high a tension as it can stand; then tune the remaining three, as I will now freely show you.

Concerning the tuning of the other three strings.

1. Tune
2. the
3. open

{ e / b♮ / G } to the { fingered b♮ [on the ā string] a fifth higher.[131] / open e a fourth higher. / fingered c [on the b♮ string] a fourth higher. }

Or tune the strings thus, as the letters show here.[132]

Another tuning method

Example

All open:
{ 1. ā / 2. e / 3. b♮ / 4. G } { fourth / fourth / major third }

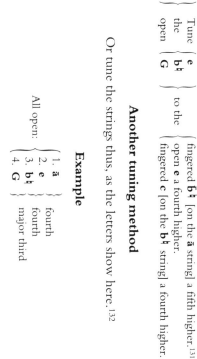

How the tenor or alto is correctly tuned from the treble.

When the treble is tuned, then tune the others with skill also, as I will teach you below. You must strive to attain this.

How the bass is tuned to the tenor

1 / 2 / 3 / 4 — To the
- open e
- open a
- open ā
- fingered c [on the G string]

in the treble tune the
- fingered e [on the d string]
- open a
- open E
- open C

in the tenor at the
- unison.
- lower octave.
- lower octave.
- lower octave.

1 / 2 / 3 — To the
- fingered b♮ [on the a string]
- open a
- open E

in the tenor tune the
- open b♮
- fingered a [on the G string]
- fingered E [on the D string]
- open A

in the bass at the
- unison.
- unison.
- unison.
- lower octave.

1 / 2 / 3 / 4 / 5 — To the
- open a
- open E
- fingered F [on the E string]

in the bass tune the
- open A
- fingered F [on the E string]

- lower octave.
- lower octave.

Concerning the small three-string hand-fiddle.

At the same time you should observe further that there is yet another type of fiddle, which is tuned in fifths in the Polish manner. It is proper, however, to finger it differently, as will be better revealed below. I also observe this generally: everyone now wants to occupy himself with it, but few understand the neck, on which the correct foundation is concealed and quite suitable. The fingerings of the musical notes [*des gesangs schlüssel*] remind me of a bowl in which there is a covered dinner, and no one can say whether it is a tasty meal or a common one such as rice, buttermilk[133] or thick whey, which the peasants like to strain. You must not think ill of me because I talk like a farmer,[134] for take note here of the proverb 'Let a cobbler stick to his last.'[135]

But when the cover is removed, then everyone recognises quickly what was lying concealed therein. It is the same thing here, as I tell you.

Therefore, in a short time below, I will artfully uncover and present to you what is hidden on these fiddles without frets. You will find both types clearly revealed in the diagrams, for they have one practice, both the Polish and the small type, except that the Polish players in fact place their fingers between the strings and stop them with their nails at the places where the frets actually should be.

The fingers must be held above [the strings] on the aforementioned little fiddles. Also, because no frets are set on them, each finger controls two positions, as I shall illustrate clearly for you in the diagrams by means of the numbers placed on the right side. There you have the basic information.

There follow three other masterly diagrams, in which the method of the Polish fiddle and the small unfretted fiddle, on which the strings are tuned in fifths, is clearly displayed.

The neck of the treble[136]

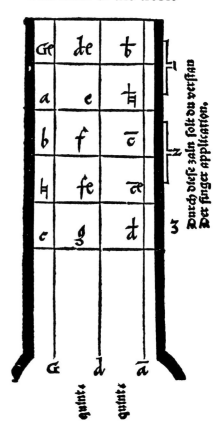

(*Right:* Understand the application of the fingers by means of these numbers. *Bottom:* Fifth. Fifth.)

Concerning the transverse lines.

The transverse lines are drawn onto the neck with a pen and show where the fingering positions are, which are otherwise recognised by means of the frets – as I shall artfully report below. Therefore, let this be commended to you.

The neck of the tenor-and-alto[137]

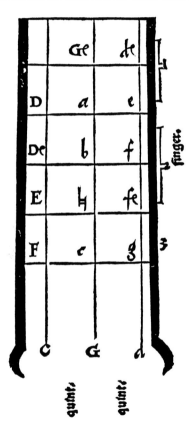

(*Right:* Fingers. *Bottom:* Fifth. Fifth.)

107

The neck of the bass[138]

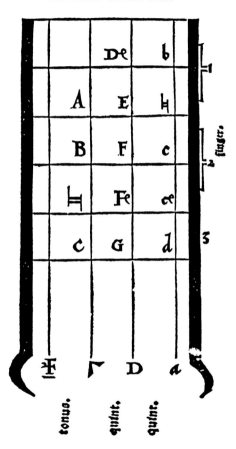

	Dᶜ	b
A	E	♮
B	F	c
♮	Fᵉ	cᵉ
c	G	d

tonus.   quint.   quint.

(Right: Fingers. *Bottom:* Whole-tone. Fifth. Fifth.)

You should also now know this: that some players tune the bass a fifth below the tenor.[139] Everyone does as he wishes, but in my opinion this seems to be the best method.

Four small fiddles without frets and with three strings[140]

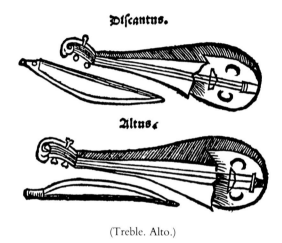

Discantus.

Altus.

(Treble. Alto.)

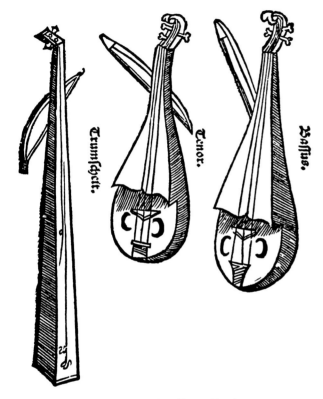

(Trumpet marine. Tenor. Bass.)

There follows another diagram, showing how the fingerings of the Polish fiddle or small three-string, unfretted fiddle tuned in fifths are measured out with the dividers.

If you want to have the method of both of the fiddles just mentioned, then draw simple letters on them, which correctly yield the fingerings, measured out indeed with the dividers as I have explained here. What I shall say concerning the treble, do also with the other necks.

A fine diagram showing the measuring off of the treble.

fol. 49ᵛ: sig. Gᵛ   The second chapter

fol. 50: sig. G2   *Concerning three kinds of fiddles*

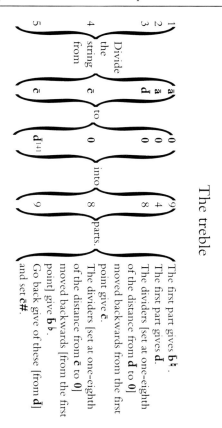

[See Appendix 22 for a table of intervals derived from the instructions for measuring off the necks of the large Italian fiddle, the Polish fiddle and the small three-string, unfretted fiddle, found on fols. 41, 41ᵛ, 42 and 49ᵛ.]

Concerning the other necks.

In measuring, continue in the same way with the tenor, the bass and also the alto. Nevertheless, hear correctly the opinion that each voice [i.e., size of fiddle] should have the letters [*buchstaben*] that belong to it, as one observes above.

When the measuring off is finished, if you draw lines on the necks with your pen transversely across the established points where the letters are found, then you can get the correct fingerings; for it is very certain that they must be quite close by, as on the necks prepared in the Italian manner, which are partitioned off right at the frets.

A lesson on tuning together the three-string Polish fiddles or the small hand-fiddles.

1. Tune the highest string as high as it will go. 2. The second string is tuned a fifth lower. 3. In the same way tune the third string below the second. When the treble is tuned, you can then use it as a model. Thus, tune the others, as follows here.

How the tenor is tuned to the treble.

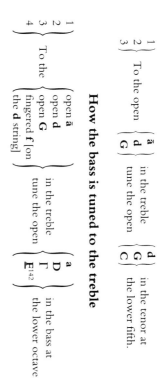

1)
2) To the open { ā / d / G } in the tenor at the lower fifth. { d / G / C }
3)

How the bass is tuned to the treble

1)
2)
3) To the { open ā / open d / open G / fingered **f** [on the **d** string] } in the bass at the lower octave. { a / D / Γ / F¹⁴² }
4)

Epilogue

That the method and ornamentation [*Coloratur*] of the organist is the best and should be employed properly on all instruments.

Although there would be still more to say here about this art, such as playing ornaments [*Colorirn*] and introducing embellishments [*Mordanten*], which decorate the melody excellently on all kinds of instruments, I cannot describe everything here at this time, however, as it would become much too long. Thus I shall abandon this merry tale.

   But if you nevertheless want to know about this, then you may have the benefit of it from a master who is skilled in instruments; he will show you thoroughly. But[143] take this advice from me: imitate the method of the organ in playing wind instruments, fiddles, lutes and whatever others can be mentioned, for I say at this time that this[144] is the best method for playing ornaments and also fast passages [*Risswerck*]. Therefore practise this usage well.

The third chapter: a short and understandable instruction on the artful measuring off of the frets on lutes and the monochord, which is very necessary for all lutenists, also fiddlers etc., to know.

Further, several important matters deriving out of the things mentioned above should be noted here. You should also have the benefit of them from me. Comprehend very well this account of how to prepare the neck on the lute and, similarly, on fiddles in general. This will be the correct opinion.

   If you wish to set the frets correctly, then[145] attend to the matter in this way.

   If you divide off the highest string by itself, then the frets will coincide on all of the other strings. You should prepare it thus.

   At[146] the highest end, **g** is drawn; underneath, at the bridge [*querholtz*], **0** is placed. And pay attention diligently to this account of where the dividers are to start. This is carried out right at the nut [*höltzlein*], where the parting of the string takes place, and the division must continue on down to the[147] place where the strings are fastened [i.e., the bridge]. You must also take care that the dividers maintain their course, for one notices very precisely when the division is incorrect by only a tiny amount.

Also[148] notice one thing in addition: where the letters are located, inscribe a point with the dividers and always keep it in mind. If you wish to pursue this correctly, look at the following diagram.

The diagram of the measuring out of the lute neck

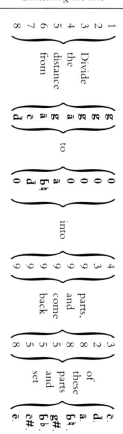

[See Appendix 23 for a table of intervals derived from these instructions for setting frets on the neck of the lute.]

What is to be accomplished further.

Now when the division is finished, lay the frets down cross-wise, running over the neck, right on the points of the letters.

When you start at the top, the frets should always get smaller [i.e., the gut strands thinner] as they go down. After that you may occupy yourself further with directing the correct letters adroitly under the other strings, as shown below very clearly on the lute neck at the end of the discussion, which you will find without any risk. From this it is easy to understand how transcribing for lutes is accomplished according to the correct method – I say this to you at this time. Thus the lute is correctly prepared; observe this from a faithful servant.

According to this method, as now reported, all lute and fiddle frets can be properly placed, thus avoiding many shallow, false fifths [*schale rossquint*], which those who do not arrange the frets correctly often have to pinch [*zwicken*].[149]

The fact that the majority of the brotherhood of lutenists and fiddlers make all of the frets the same [distance] from each other[150]

is truly a telling indication of their great inexperience – of the fact that they have no knowledge of the science that noble Music proclaims. Thus they too go astray, for they understand nothing at all about how the division of the whole-tone is accomplished. They also do not know that a fret that produces a minor semitone[151] should stand somewhat farther [back] from the following [higher] fret, for the closest fret [i.e., the one for the lower pitch of the minor semitone, placed at the back of the first fret in question] takes precedence. Thus the major semitone is indeed somewhat larger than the minor semitone, for the major has five commas [*Commata*] and the minor only four, as the monochord displays: there one perceives how a comparison is made.

Concerning the whole-tone division, the two semitones and the comma.

The whole-tone, or major second, consists of two semitones, a major one and a minor one. The major semitone comprises five commas, and the minor four. Moreover, the comma is the smallest interval, nine of which constitute a complete whole-tone.

Here is the correct, musical and new
tablature, written on the lute neck, from
which one easily learns to transcribe for
the lute.

The musical lute neck[152]

A diagram of the unisons or identically sounding letters on the lute neck, very necessary to know in transcribing.

(*Across the middle:* This . . . sounds the same as this . . . and this . . . the same as this.)

Concerning tuning the lute down

Many pieces of vocal music are composed that reach [down to] **Ff** under **Γ**, which cannot be played conveniently according to the illustrated lute neck unless one makes use of what is called tuning the lute down, namely when the lowest course is set one tone lower than before. Because this is difficult to play, I think the best method is to have the lute prepared, strung with thirteen strings, on which one can play such a piece of music, as this diagram shows.[153]

When the lute is tuned down

The lowest open string gives **Ff**, the first fret **Ff#**, the second **G**, the third **G#**, the fourth **A** (believe this indeed), the fifth **B♭**, the sixth **B♮** and the seventh **C**.

A second lute neck, on which thirteen strings are strung and the musical tablature is applied, together with the old tablature[154]

How good strings on instruments strung with gut strings – such as lutes, fiddles, harps, psalteries, hurdy-gurdies [*Leyrn*] etc. – are recognised and selected.[155]

When you open up a small bundle, take the string that is as long as it should be (measure it out on the instrument), and do not forget what follows here: stretch it between your separated hands, and strike it solely with your third finger[156] so that it vibrates and hums well. Observe diligently what results from this: the smaller the reaction there, the better the string – believe me truly. Conversely, the greater the reverberation, the worse the string, as I tell you. Such a string as just mentioned can never be set right. Therefore you must select it well if it is to sound pure and correct.

How the selected strings are correctly allotted and ordered into the six courses of the lute.

1.[158] For the **G**[159] take a coarse string. 2.[160] The **C** is a little smaller. 3.[161] The **F**, however, is finer. Also, I tell you at this time that a moderate-sized string at the octave belongs to each course [mentioned above]. 4.[162] String the **a** with two medium-sized strings, so that they are the same in sound. 5.[163] String the **d** also as just described, but in a smaller size. 6.[164] To the **g** belongs the very smallest, and it should be the purest of all, for if it is false, I tell you freely, it will spoil the entire melody.

How the strings are first arranged on the
lute, how two are individually strung
together for each course, and how they
are tuned by fourths and a third, as is
now the practice.

At this time lutenists tune lutes by the following methods.
First, the **g** must be as high as it can possibly stand. The
interval of the fourth produces **d** from **g** and **a** from **d**; the
third produces **F** from **a**. The fourth provides **C** from **F** and
G[165] from **C**. Thus they are all correctly set. There follows a
little diagram of this showing how they are all to be tuned.

There follows the first diagram of the
tuning up [*auffzihn*] of the strings.

Tuning up the lute strings[166]

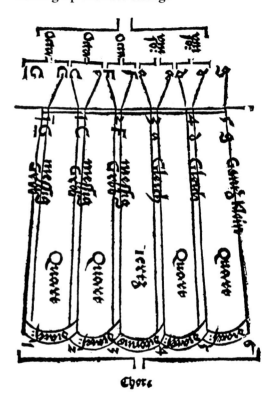

(*Far-left column:* Unison. Unison. Octave. Octave. Octave. *Left-centre column:* Very small. The same. The same. Moderate; thick. Moderate; thick. Moderate; thick. *Right-centre column:* Fourth. Fourth. Third. Fourth. Fourth. *Right column:* Fourth. Fourth. Major third. Fourth. Fourth. *Far right:* Course.)

A second method, easier and more refined than the previous one, of tuning the strings correctly by octaves

Because the kind of tuning that we have taught up to now is very difficult, especially for schoolboys who have not done much singing, I will therefore announce an easier method using octaves, which seldom fails. For an octave is, in truth, far easier than thirds and fourths, as a musician must admit. It is hardly necessary to say this.

Now follows the easy method of tuning the lute at this time. 1. Tune the highest string as high as you can without its breaking when you pluck it. 2. Fingered **G** [on the **F** string] must sound an octave lower than open **g**.

3		**G**[167]			lower			**G** [on the **F** string].
4	Tune	**a**	an		lower	than		**ā** [on the **g** string].
5	the	**C**	octave		lower	the		**c** [on the **a** string].
6	open	**d**			higher	fingered		**D**[168] [on the **C** string].

You need not question any further, for they are all correctly tuned. There follows a fine little diagram of this; adhere to it in every endeavour. It was presented to me by dear Music – my heart and soul are devoted to her – so that I may now bestow it on you. She will yet give me much more.

There follows the second diagram showing how the strings are to be tuned easily by octaves. [See Appendices 24 and 18.]

A little diagram of the names and symbols for the instrumental semitones that belong to musica ficta [i.e., the chromatic notes].

$$
\left.\begin{matrix} \mathbf{C} \\ \mathbf{D} \\ \mathbf{G} \\ \mathbf{F} \end{matrix}\right\} \text{ signifies } \left\{\begin{matrix} \mathbf{D}\,\flat \\ \mathbf{E}\,\flat \\ \mathbf{a}\,\flat \\ \mathbf{G}\,\flat \end{matrix}\right\} \text{ and the same is true of their octaves.}
$$

Lauten. [169]

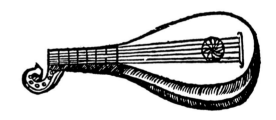

Quintern.

(Lute. Gittern.)

More concerning the lute at another time.

Concerning the measuring off and preparing of the instrument called the monochord [*Monochordum*], in which is contained much concealed science applicable to music and all instruments, written very concisely in rhyme.

'Monochord'[170] is the name given to a quadrangular, hollow instrument with one string, approximately six spans[171] long and a half-span[172] wide (observe this at the beginning), on which intervals – with which music is concerned – are artfully divided off by means of the dividers so that not even a hair's breadth is lacking. The ancients held it in great esteem long ago; with it, schoolboys first mastered the notes in singing as required for each interval [*Modus*]. Thus, the practice of using it was increased, as the teachings of Guido [of Arezzo]

and other writers show us.

For when it is prepared correctly, it shows clearly and genuinely how each interval sounds and how the leaps are sung. It is also easy to perceive, if one wants to model the clavichord and the like on it correctly, whether these instruments deviate from each other with regard to their methods, as derived from the monochord. Do not let these words displease you. The proportions and the little pins [*bretlein*] to which the keys [*Claves*] are attached within the body of the clavichord must also be placed and measured just as on the monochord. Indeed, the tangents [*Tangenten*] fastened onto the keys [*Clavim*] should stand directly against the division points if the division is to come about correctly. When this arrangement is correctly carried out, a proper sound will be produced.

Further, one should know in this respect that from this proceed all instruments, such as organs, wind instruments (as I say), and many more that can be named; for the way this practice is carried out also applies to fingerholes on winds and to the lute neck, as reported above, and it also holds true on fiddles and on others, in addition, about which I cannot speak now. The following accounts, however, show thoroughly how it is prepared.

There follows the division.

1.

First[173] place a point at the beginning [of the string], likewise an **F**,[174] the letter [*Schlüssel*] directly underneath Γ, at the very same place. Establish this and remember it. Next, with a **0**,[175] identify the end [of the string] as indeed the limit of all of the measuring. A little point placed in the centre [of the **0**] is considered the correct destination point [*zylmass*]. Draw[176] a line from it to the **F**[177] on which all of the points will be placed. Do not let go of the dividers, for they always show the correct measurement. For this reason they are called a master of science; without them all division is in vain.

Finally, divide the length from **F**[178] to **0** into nine equal parts. At the [end of the] first part [i.e., the point of division between the first and second parts], Γ is written, and at the [end of the] third part **C** is placed; **G** is to stand at the [end of the] fifth, **c** at the [end of the] sixth, and **g** at the [end of the] seventh. Let the other parts stand unused, and see how you proceed henceforth.

2.

Divide the preceding length into eight parts and gain **B**♭ at the [end of the] second. You will get **F** at the [end of the] fourth and **b**♭ at the [end of the] fifth. Obtain **f** at the [end of the] sixth and **ff** at the [end of the] seventh.

3.

Make nine areas from Γ to **0**. **A** is placed at the [end of the] first, **D** at the [end of the] third, **a** at the [end of the] fifth, and **d** solely at the [end of the] sixth. The place for **aa** is the [end of the] seventh.

4.

Partition **A** to **0** into nine parts. Place **B**♮ at the [end of the] first and **E** at the [end of the] third. The [end of the] fifth has to do with **b**♮ and the [end of the] sixth with **e**. At the [end of the] seventh, **bb**♮ is found.

5.

In the middle between $\left\{\begin{matrix}\mathbf{c}\\\mathbf{d}\\\mathbf{e}\end{matrix}\right\}$ and **0**, place $\left\{\begin{matrix}\mathbf{cc.}\\\mathbf{dd.}\\\mathbf{ee.}\end{matrix}\right\}$

Truly indeed, every octave is measured out by means of a dupla proportion ($\frac{2}{1}$); thus the octave is often called 'dupla', as is known to the theorists [*den Theoricis*].

Concerning the attributes of the semitones.

6.

Divide **B♮** to **0** into ten parts. The[180] [end of the] first confirms **C#**, the [end of the] second **D#**. The [end of the] fourth receives **G#**, the [end of the] sixth **d#**. The [end of the] seventh fits with **g#**, the [end of the] eighth with **dd#**.

7.

C# to **0** is made into eight parts. At the [end of the] second, **F#** is produced, and at the [end of the] fourth, **c#**. At the [end of the] fifth, **f#** is placed, and at the [end of the] sixth, **cc#**. This is considered a proper division.

8.

Finally, **bb♭** is also essential and is perceived in the middle between **b♭** and **0**. Thus the division is completed, and this instrument is made correct.[181] If you want to investigate all of this, then fasten a string on it and insert a bridge [*höltzlein*] over the first **F**[182] so that it comes into contact with the string above it. It should stand in the middle on the point, so that the correct length will be established, and likewise on the **0** at the [other] end. Then[183] draw a bridge adroitly up to the string, placing it on the string at any letter you please, and let the string vibrate thoroughly

so that the sound can be distinguished. Do this on the right side [i.e., allow the string to vibrate between the movable bridge and the fixed bridge identified with the figure **0**] (this is said to you without any frivolity), and you will surely hear and perceive the pitch of the note [*des Schlüssels melodey*]. You will not make even the slightest mistake; attempt it and you will experience it for a fact. I surely would have said much about this if it had been suitable for this purpose – about what kind of usefulness it harbours that can be employed skilfully in the study of theory [*zur Theorick*] and other things that pertain to music; but the matter may rest until I write more about it. Therefore be satisfied now with this, until I add more for you.

[See Appendix 26 for a table of intervals derived from the instructions for setting the notes on the monochord according to two methods: (1) as presented on fols. 61ᵛ–63, and (2) as presented on the foldout cited on fol. 63ᵛ, and on fols. 64–64ᵛ.]

There follows, further, an artful diagram showing how every octave is basically measured out individually on the monochord according to the proportions of the Pythagorean hammers.

𝕬𝖓𝖕𝖔𝖘 𝖒𝖎𝖙 𝕯𝖊𝖒𝖒𝖊𝖗𝖓. [184]

(Anvil with hammers.)

In this diagram you can see how the division is to be carried out according to the four hammers (observe this), as Pythagoras teaches us. [See Appendix 25.]

Concerning the adding of the other semitones.

10.[185]

Make[186] two equal parts from **D#** to **0**. Place the dividers [set to the measurement of one of these parts], according to their method, on **D#** and let them go down [in the direction of **E**]. Thus you will see that **G#** should stand there.

11.

Divide[187] **G#** to **0**, according to this proportion, into four equal parts (I say briefly). Go back three of these parts to the right [i.e., in the direction of **0**] and you will find where **C#** should stand.

12.

Divide **C#** to **0** into two parts. Let the dividers [set to the measurement of one of these parts] hang down very quickly [in the direction of **F**] from the **C#**, and you will be able to attain the **F#**.[188] The lowest end [of the dividers] will quickly report where the specific position of the pitch is.

Thus, an entire octave is divided off, adorned with all of its semitones. Do the same when you want to go higher and tackle the other octaves. Nevertheless I will instruct you in the way you should accomplish this quickly. Divide the distance from **0** to each pitch in the first octave into two equal parts;

and[189] a letter placed at the middle will be considered the octave above. For example, if you want to get the octave above **A** (which is called **a**) readily, make two parts from **A** to **0**, and place **a** there at the midpoint. Do the same with the others that go up an octave higher. When the second octave is accomplished, then I take refuge even further in the third octave. I consider that this is made according to the second octave, and the fourth according to the third. Do the same in further stages: when you want to add more octaves, you must follow this procedure.

[See Appendix 26 for a table of intervals derived from the instructions for setting the notes on the monochord according to two methods: (1) as presented on fols. 61ᵛ–63, and (2) as presented on the foldout cited on fol. 63ᵛ, and on fols. 64–64ᵛ.]

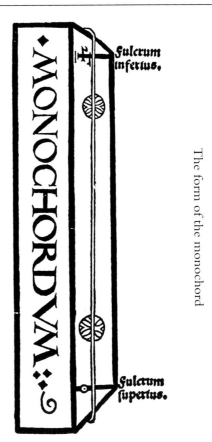

(*Top right:* The lower bridge. *Bottom right:* The upper bridge.)

The fourth chapter, concerning the four Pythagorean hammers, together with their proportions, from which much useful science arises, such as the dividing off of the fiddle and lute necks and the monochord, as described above, and also the length and width of organ pipes and the artful tuning of small bells [*Zimbeln*] or bells [*Glöcklein*] etc., as follows.

Preface

The master called Pythagoras was well known in the science of mathematics and likewise in music, as the following evidence indicates.

At his time, people had a very obscure understanding of music, for it was not as clear to them as it now is to us – believe me truly. Therefore[191] he speculated for many hours in order to discover the correct foundation of this music, noble and fine – how sounds came about according to speculative method. And he became certain of the matter, namely what kind of proportion is produced by a high and a low tone when they are assessed together, about which the theorists have babbled.

Well then, perhaps God moved him to[192] go out walking one day, and he came to the door of a blacksmith, where he heard an unusual sound, struck simply with the hammers on the iron by the smith's helpers, who struck the anvil so swiftly that sparks flew all over. He stood with his ears pricked up and thought, 'This will indeed not be wasted, but will yet turn out for the best.' And he pondered in his mind, as the hammers were sounding together, one big and the other small, 'Why indeed does it appear that they make such different sounds?'

In[193] fact, he heard a whole-tone [*Tonum*], a fourth [*Diatessaron*], a fifth [*Diapent*] and an octave [*Diapason*] sounding there, and he thought, 'I am really surprised. Perhaps, in this procedure, it depends on the strength of the smith's helpers.' Then he quickly had the hammers changed, letting each man wield one other than he had done previously; and he ordered them to strike boldly. He let the hammers remain those that the men had used previously, except that they were exchanged and somewhat differently managed.

As he then listened at length and did not perceive any sounds other than those that had been made previously, he thought, 'How indeed can this be? Since it does not depend on the arms [of the men], there must be another reason. Perhaps it is the weights of the hammers that cause them to sound in this way.' Then he tried another trick: he had the hammer handles knocked out and the four irons weighed by themselves, and he waited to see what would happen. Only then did he discover the correct plan, which[194] is called theoretical speculation – namely a product of the weights of the hammers prepared in proportions,

such as dupla ($\frac{12}{6}$), sesquialtera ($\frac{9}{6}$), sesquitertia ($\frac{12}{9}$) and sesquioctava ($\frac{9}{8}$). These were indeed the weights of the four hammers, quite clearly.

An[195] octave was heard between the first and the fourth hammers in dupla proportion. The[196] first and the third, called sesquialtera, clearly sounded a fifth. The[197] first and the second, sesquitertia, gave a fourth without any jest. The[198] second and the third, sesquioctava, provided a whole-tone.

Thus, as appears here below, he discovered the four intervals [*Modos*] – whole-tone, fourth, fifth and octave – and[199] what the proportion of each one is, as theoretical speculation freely teaches. He was the first to discover this, as it seems to me. Manifold arts proceed from it, as is described here to some degree. Look first at this diagram[200] and then at the other things I shall bring forth.

Concerning the remaining things, Macrobius, in book 2 of the [Commentary on the] Dream of Scipio, says the following.[201]

And when Pythagoras had recorded the difference in the weight of each hammer, he had other hammers heavier or lighter than these made. Blows from these produced sounds that were not at all like those of the original hammers, and besides, consonant sounds were not heard. He then concluded that harmony of tones was produced according to a proportion of the weights, and he made a record of all the numerical relations of the various weights producing harmony. Next he directed his investigation from hammers to stringed instruments and stretched intestines of sheep and sinews of oxen by attaching to them weights of the same proportions as those determined by the hammers. Again the concord came forth that had been assured by his earlier well-conceived experiment, but with a sweeter tone, as we might expect from the nature of stringed instruments, etc.

The first diagram of the four hammers, in which their proportions are correctly measured out on four lines.

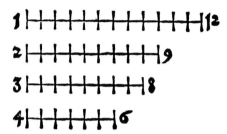

Here Pythagoras weighs the four hammers.[202]

There follows the second diagram, in which the form of the four Pythagorean hammers, together with their proportions, is quite clearly conceived and illustrated, theoretically and practically.

(*Top:* Octave: dupla. *Across the middle top:* Fifth: sesquialtera. Fifth: sesquialtera. *Across the lower top:* Fourth: sesquitertia. Sesquioctava: whole-tone. Sesquitertia: fourth. *Across the upper bottom:* Sesquitertia: fourth. Whole-tone. Fourth. *Across the middle bottom*: Fifth. Fifth. *Bottom:* Octave: dupla.)

The description of proportion

Proportion,²⁰⁴ according to common experience, is the comparing together of two things that are of the same kind, such as number with number (remember this) and line with line; add also body with body, note with note, and sound with sound, as is observed in music, both contrapuntal and theoretical [*Figral und Theorica*]. Read on and you will find this here.

Further,²⁰⁵ do not let it vex you that I shall conclude so quickly and not say anything here about dividing proportions, and also not indicate how many categories of proportions there are. I consider this not necessary now, because I described it clearly in the past in²⁰⁶ a German Measured [Music].²⁰⁷ There you will find enough about this. Therefore we want to let this stand here and, for the sake of brevity, write only about what will be necessary to us.

Concerning adding proportions.

If[208] you want to speculate further and add proportion to proportion, then reduce them to their smallest numbers, as I shall instruct here below. After that, they are then added the way fractions are multiplied, the[209] denominator by the denominator and the numerator by the numerator – this is the way it is done.

The adding of the proportions hemiola [i.e., sesquialtera] and sesquitertia.

For[210] example, should you want to add sesquialtera proportion to[211] sesquitertia (in music this is the fifth to the fourth, just as I understand it), then reduce both proportions to the smallest, very concise numbers – for[212] example, sesquialtera thus: $\frac{3}{2}$, and sesquitertia[213] like this: $\frac{4}{3}$. Then say, '3 times 4 gives 12, and 2 times 3 is certainly 6.' Thus,[214] from this, dupla (called the octave in music) is produced. If you do the same with the others, you will follow this practice correctly.

Another example, showing how sesquitertia [i.e., the fourth] is added to tripla [i.e., the twelfth].

numerators:	multiply 4 and 3	}	the result is quadruple	}	12 3	}	in music, the double octave.

A brief annotation

In the addition of proportions, the numerator of one of them is multiplied by the numerator of the other, and the denominator of one by the denominator of the other.

Concerning subtracting proportions.

If[215] you want to subtract a proportion from a proportion in the correct manner, then observe this. Start with the smallest number of each proportion; then follow the same procedure as with dividing fractions.

Simply multiply the denominator of one proportion exactly crosswise by the other numerator, and then the converse. Thus this is clear.

For example, if you now want to subtract sesquialtera $\frac{3}{2}$ from tripla $\frac{3}{1}$ (in music this is subtracting the fifth from the interval known as the twelfth), say, '3 times 1 gives only 3, and 2 times 3 is simply 6.' Following this procedure, the result is dupla $\frac{6}{3}$, which I call the octave in music. Do the same with the others, and you will not deviate from the fundamentals.

Another example, showing how sesquialtera [i.e., the fifth] is subtracted from dupla [i.e., the octave].

numerators: 3   *mul ti ply*   2   } the result is sesquitertia   { 4 3 }   in music, the fourth.

denominators: 2   *mul ti ply*   1

sesquialtera   dupla   sesquitertia

Supplement

In the subtraction of proportions, the numerator of one proportion and the denominator of the other are always multiplied crosswise.

How all proportions that are large are to be reduced to smaller numbers, which is very useful to know for the adding and subtracting of proportions.[216]

If you desire, in these matters, to make a proportion smaller (which is very necessary to observe in conjunction with the procedures described here), then subtract the smaller number from the larger one in continued reduction, as often (I say) as it is possible. Pay close attention to me in these matters. Do this with both numbers, from one to the next, and it will proceed correctly to the point where they are both equal. Thus you indeed have your instructions.

Then divide both numbers of the first proportion by this concise number. The quotient will tell clearly what[217] the smallest number of the proportion is. Let us prove with sesquitertia how to proceed with this pleasantry.

An example of sesquitertia

In $\frac{16}{12}$, subtract 12 from 16 and 4 remains; thus $\frac{4}{12}$ results. Then subtract 4 from 12 and 8 remains; thus $\frac{4}{8}$ results. Finally, subtract 4 from 8 and 4 remains; the result is that both are equal, thus $\frac{4}{4}$. Now divide the previous two numbers, 16 and 12, by 4, and say, '4 into 16 goes 4 times, and 4 into 12 goes 3 times.' Thus the very smallest number of sesquitertia is produced, namely $\frac{4}{3}$.

Do the same with the other proportions, and you will pursue the matter correctly.

A diagram in which the proportions of the higher and lower pitches of various musical intervals are very clearly conceived according to speculative method.[218]

1[219]	Comma	524288:531441
2	Minor semitone[220]	243:256
3	Major semitone[221]	2048:2187
4	Whole-tone	8:9
5	Minor third [*Semiditonus*]	27:32
6	Major third [*Ditonus*]	64:81
7	Fourth	3:4
8	Augmented fourth [*Tritonus*]	512:729
9	Diminished fifth [*Semidiapent.*][222]	729:1024
10	Fifth	2:3
11	Minor sixth [*Se.to.diapent.*]	81:128
12	Major sixth [*To.diapent.*]	16:27
13	Minor seventh [*Se.dit.diapent.*]	9:16
14	Major seventh [*Dit.diapent.*]	128:243
15[223]	Octave	1:2
16	Octave and a [minor] semitone	243:512[224]
17	Octave and a whole-tone	4:9
18	Octave and a minor third	27:64
19	Octave and a major third	32:81
20	Octave and a fourth	3:8
21	Octave and an augmented fourth	256:729
22	Octave and a diminished fifth	729:2048[225]
23	Octave and a fifth	2:6[226]
24	Octave and a minor sixth	81:256
25	Octave and a major sixth	8:27
26	Octave and a minor seventh	9:32
27	Octave and a major seventh	64:243
28[227]	Double-octave	1:4
29	Double-octave and a [minor] semitone	243:1024
30	Double-octave and a whole-tone	8:36[228]

31	Double-octave and a minor third	27:128
32	Double-octave and a major third	64:324[229]
33	Double-octave and a fourth	3:16
34	Double-octave and an augmented fourth	512:2916[230]
35	Double-octave and a fifth	2:12[231]
36	Double-octave and a minor sixth	81:512
37	Double-octave and a major sixth	16:108[232]
38	Double-octave and a minor seventh	9:64
39	Double-octave and a major seventh	128:972[233]
40[234]	Triple-octave	1:8
41	Triple-octave and a whole-tone	1:9
42	Triple-octave and a fourth	3:32
43	Triple-octave and a fifth	1:12
44[235]	Quadruple-octave	1:16[236]

The proportions of the remaining intervals may be discovered with no difficulty by adding what is missing in the above.

An artful speculation on how organ pipes are quite thoroughly and scientifically tuned, before their metal [*blech*] is soldered together, by means of the theoretical proportions of the musical intervals, which is useful for all organ makers and other elegant, clever and speculating minds.

Since I have described something here about the Pythagorean hammers and their proportions and musical sounds, from which many other arts arise, such as how one correctly tunes organ pipes and also other kinds of wind instruments, and likewise small bells [*zimbeln*] etc.; therefore, so that I might give a reason for speculating further to boys and others who would have a desire for such scientific matters, I will now consider the two matters – the tuning of organ pipes and bells [*Glöcklein*] – separately and treat them here in the briefest way, as much as is appropriate, and then conclude my book.

Concerning the tuning of organ pipes.

First, if you want to employ this method of tuning correctly, then you[237] must know well the rule of three [*Regulam di tre*] and also, as presented above, the proportions of the intervals. For example, if you have a piece of metal for an organ pipe that is 12 spans[238] long and 2 spans wide, and if you want to know the length and width of the metal for a second pipe tuned a fifth above (which is sesquialtera proportion, $\frac{3}{2}$), then place the upper number of the proportion (3) at the beginning in the rule, the lower number (2) in the middle, and the number of spans in the first piece of metal (12) at the end. Thus, the [239] length is first figured in this way:

The rule of three applied to the length.

3   2   12

Then multiply and divide, saying, '2 times 12 is 24; now 3 into 24 goes 8 times.' Thus you have the length of the second pipe that is tuned a fifth higher, namely 8 spans. Then[240] consider the width, 2 spans, and place it into the rule of three thus:

The rule of three applied to the width.

3[241]   2   2
spans

And say, '2 times 2 is 4, and 3 into 4 goes once, with one left over, otherwise expressed in fractions as one-third.' Thus you have the width, as follows.

An example

The $\begin{cases} \text{first} \\ \\ \text{second} \end{cases}$ piece of metal is $\begin{cases} 12 \\ \\ 8 \end{cases}$ spans long and $\begin{cases} 2 \\ \\ 1\frac{1}{3}\,^{242} \end{cases}$ spans wide.

Thus proceed with all other pipes as in this diagram, in which an octave, tuned and defined, is clearly revealed.

There follows the diagram of the measuring of the metal for the organ pipes that constitute an octave, such as from Γ to G.

A brief annotation

To add the other notes above, the octave placed below should be halved, and it is done in this way.

Example

$$\left.\begin{array}{l}\textbf{c:}\\\textbf{C:}\end{array}\right\} \quad \text{length:} \quad \left\{\begin{array}{l}6\\12\end{array}\right\} \quad \text{width:} \quad \left\{\begin{array}{l}1\tfrac{1}{2}\\3\end{array}\right\}$$

Do the others in a similar way. [See Appendix 27.]

In addition

Whatever there may be to say about this secret art in addition, such as the casting and soldering together of the metal, also the length and width of the lip [*des labials*] etc., I want to recommend to other artists and practitioners of this art, who, although they are obliged to communicate this to their neighbour according to Christian practice, generally 'keep hidden behind the mountain', as is said. And because they take the art with them to the grave, they serve only themselves in this way, and not their neighbour. Enough said; everyone can behave as if he knows how he will answer God when He says to him:

Give an account of thy stewardship, and of thy talents[243] etc.

More concerning the organ at another time.

There follows, further, a second fine speculation and correct model showing how bells or small bells and also other sounding metal [*metall*] are tuned and prepared by weight, according to the Pythagorean and speculative method.

A brief annotation

Just as the dividers are the master of the science of things to be measured, so also can the rule of three be called the master of things to be counted.

If you want to pursue this tuning correctly, then proceed by placing the numbers of the weights and proportions into the rule of three, as stated above concerning the organ pipes. Concerning this, see the diagram placed below.

A diagram in which three octaves of tuned small bells are conceived.[244]

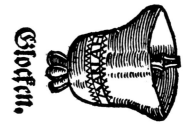

(*Top:* Small bells. *Bottom left:* Bell.)

The diagram follows.[245]

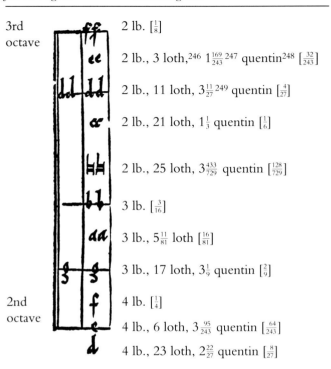

3rd octave

2 lb. $\left[\frac{1}{8}\right]$

2 lb., 3 loth,[246] $1\frac{169}{243}$ [247] quentin[248] $\left[\frac{32}{243}\right]$

2 lb., 11 loth, $3\frac{11}{27}$ [249] quentin $\left[\frac{4}{27}\right]$

2 lb., 21 loth, $1\frac{1}{3}$ quentin $\left[\frac{1}{6}\right]$

2 lb., 25 loth, $3\frac{433}{729}$ quentin $\left[\frac{128}{729}\right]$

3 lb. $\left[\frac{3}{16}\right]$

3 lb., $5\frac{11}{81}$ loth $\left[\frac{16}{81}\right]$

3 lb., 17 loth, $3\frac{1}{9}$ quentin $\left[\frac{2}{9}\right]$

2nd octave

4 lb. $\left[\frac{1}{4}\right]$

4 lb., 6 loth, $3\frac{95}{243}$ quentin $\left[\frac{64}{243}\right]$

4 lb., 23 loth, $2\frac{22}{27}$ quentin $\left[\frac{8}{27}\right]$

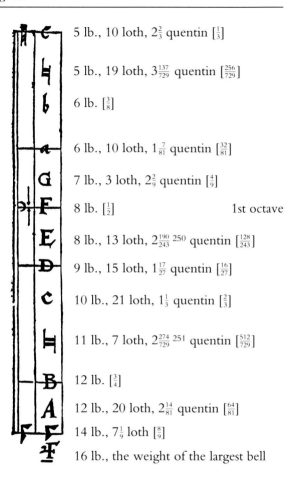

5 lb., 10 loth, $2\frac{2}{3}$ quentin $\left[\frac{1}{3}\right]$

5 lb., 19 loth, $3\frac{137}{729}$ quentin $\left[\frac{256}{729}\right]$

6 lb. $\left[\frac{3}{8}\right]$

6 lb., 10 loth, $1\frac{7}{81}$ quentin $\left[\frac{32}{81}\right]$

7 lb., 3 loth, $2\frac{2}{9}$ quentin $\left[\frac{4}{9}\right]$

8 lb. $\left[\frac{1}{2}\right]$ 1st octave

8 lb., 13 loth, $2\frac{190}{243}$ [250] quentin $\left[\frac{128}{243}\right]$

9 lb., 15 loth, $1\frac{17}{27}$ quentin $\left[\frac{16}{27}\right]$

10 lb., 21 loth, $1\frac{1}{3}$ quentin $\left[\frac{2}{3}\right]$

11 lb., 7 loth, $2\frac{274}{729}$ [251] quentin $\left[\frac{512}{729}\right]$

12 lb. $\left[\frac{3}{4}\right]$

12 lb., 20 loth, $2\frac{14}{81}$ quentin $\left[\frac{64}{81}\right]$

14 lb., $7\frac{1}{9}$ loth $\left[\frac{8}{9}\right]$

16 lb., the weight of the largest bell

The fifth chapter

There follows the tablature applied to the harp.

If you want to know the method of the harp and also, at this time, the psaltery [*Psalter*] – how their tablature is placed on the instruments pictured here, exactly as Music teaches you (you will also find the dulcimer [*Hackbret*] here) – then look at these diagrams. Here you will find it clearly presented. And although much more could still be said about this if it were appropriate, nevertheless, for the sake of brevity, I will remain silent about it for now and save it until another time, when I have more opportunity.

Die Harffe.[252]

(The harp.)

The tablature applied to the psaltery[253]

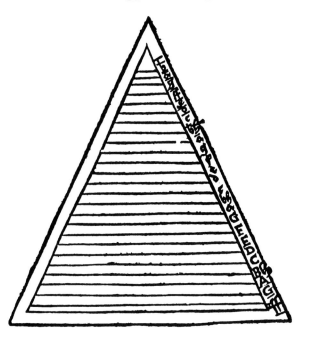

The scale or tablature applied to the xylophone[254]

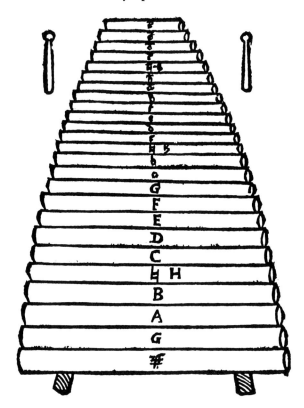

Das Hackebret.[255]

(The dulcimer.)

Conclusion

Thus[256] I want to let my book be concluded for now. In addition, I want to have requested not only you schoolchildren, my disciples, but also each and every reader of this book, that he be pleased with it (because I mean well), and that he not open up his slanderous mouth against me so wide that one could – if allowed – throw a piece of cow dung into it; rather that he consider, in case everything is perhaps not found to be discussed and prepared in the most artful way, that[257] I have never had a member[258] of the human race as an active teacher in this art during my lifetime (which certainly has been heard from me before), either in practical matters – such as plainchant, counterpoint and instrumental music – or in music theory. Rather, whatever I understand of music I received first from God, who bestows His gifts on whom He will, and then through considerably great diligence and study (although in my case solely with the help of God). Therefore I could well be called a self-made musician, and it would not be surprising if, from time to time, I did not treat important masters as equals. But I say truly that the boundless desire and love that I have had for the noble Lady[259] Music moved me to this especially solitary and secret study and,[260] just as with a rod, compelled me to it; otherwise (as every expert will acknowledge), it would have been impossible for me. For this reason, if I am at all wanting here in suitable knowledge, just bear in mind that I have nevertheless meant well with my writing up to now, even though it was not always as artful as possible, and that I still intend faithfully that it might be of service, first to God and then to my neighbour. Now if this does not please you, but you can't or won't improve on it, then consider, and plug up your shameful, slanderous mouth with a cake made of various herbs and flowers, or failure will be your just reward. All right then, my dear and well-meaning disciples and all others, I[261] ask you: help to defend me as much as you can. And since I have served you and your predecessors diligently in schools here in Magdeburg for about twenty-five or twenty-six years now and have always made do with begging so that I

could further serve you all the more suitably in this art of music, you will want to urge your parents and other concerned persons that my salary should be improved to some degree. For it is indeed written, 'The[262] labourer is worthy of his hire', and 'Who serves the altar should also live from it', and further, 'Thou[263] shalt not muzzle the mouth of the ox that treadeth out the corn', etc. Enough said: I hope that when I have been deserving, or will yet be so, you and others will still be well able to maintain my wages. Therefore take now this meagre little fish as suitable on the occasion of the new year. Now if any of you wants to put a ticket or a straw into the lottery for me for the work and expense that I have devoted to this, so that at least – if fortune should yield something – I could even win or else come into some financial aid, I will certainly permit it; and henceforth I will be very grateful in return. Now may God further you and me in our study and all godly works, and give us all eternal and joyful life after this transitory and troubled one, indeed at that place where the noble Lady Music is practised by the angels, and 'Holy, holy, holy, Lord God of Hosts' etc. is sung without ceasing. Amen.

Martin Agricola,[264]
your willing [disciple][265]

To the reader and student

Thus, my dear reader, you have the knowledge of fine instruments, namely how you should pursue[266] and begin to learn them. Now when you understand the knowledge, something even more is required: good pieces for instruments, which are seldom found in print.

For this reason (as said above), when I perceive an opportunity, and if I am requested to do so, in time I will also have some pieces printed for your use that are suitable for this purpose; you will find much of value in them that you can employ usefully.[267]

Therefore, diligently beseech God, who made heaven and earth, for grace to grant me a long, healthy life, for I still have much to give you. I did not want to conceal this, but rather declare it to you in conclusion with as many thousand farewells as are said in a year by many a laughing, red mouth.

Amen.

Printed at Wittenberg by Georg Rhau, in the year 1545.

APPENDIX 1

Table of woodcut illustrations in Agricola's *Musica instrumentalis deudsch* (1529) derived from Virdung's *Musica getutscht* (1511)

Description	Location in Agricola (fol.)	Location in Virdung (fol.)	Major differences in Agricola version
recorder	5ᵛ	Nᵛ	position of thumbhole reversed
4 recorders	8ᵛ	B3ᵛ	reversed; thumbholes shown more clearly, but relative sizes of instruments greatly changed
shawm, pommer, three-hole pipe	10ᵛ	B3ᵛ	relative positions retained, but individual items reversed
cornett	10ᵛ	B4	reversed; fingerholes moved closer to end
4 crumhorns	11	B4	reversed; instruments made shorter
bladderpipe	11	B4	reversed
curved horn	11	B4	reversed
gemshorn	11ᵛ	B4	curve of instrument made wider
rüspfeiff	11ᵛ	B4	both ends of instrument made more flaring
bagpipe	11ᵛ	B4ᵛ	reversed; proportions changed, with pipes made shorter
4 transverse flutes	13	B3ᵛ	three flutes added; reversed
trombone	16ᵛ	B4ᵛ	reversed, except for shading lines

Description	Location in Agricola (fol.)	Location in Virdung (fol.)	Major differences in Agricola version
military trumpet	16ᵛ	B4ᵛ	reversed, except for shading lines
'clareta'	16ᵛ	C (tower trumpet)	reversed, except for shading lines
'tower trumpet'	16ᵛ	C (clareta)	reversed, except for shading lines
organ	17ᵛ	Cᵛ	reversed, except for (backwards) order of keys; ornamentation above pipes changed
positive organ	18	Cᵛ	reversed (correcting original backwards order of pipes), except for (backwards) order of keys
portative organ	18	C2	reversed, except for (backwards) order of keys; 5 folds in bellows reduced to 4
regal	18ᵛ	Cᵛ	reversed
organ keyboard	26ᵛ	Gᵛ	proportions changed; different method of identifying octaves applied

145

Description	Location in Agricola (fol.)	Location in Virdung (fol.)	Major differences in Agricola version
clavichord	27	B	reversed, except for pinblock and (backwards) order of keys; extensions of keys greatly coarsened
harpsicord (clavicimbalum)	27	B^v	reversed, except for (backwards) order of keys and configuration of strings and pinblock
virginal	27^v	B^v (clavi-cymbalum)[1]	reversed, except for (backwards) order of keys
hurdy-gurdy	27^v	B^v	reversed; 8 keys increased to 11
clavicytherium	28	B^v	ornamentation above strings changed; backwards order of strings retained
lute	33	B2	reversed; 11 strings reduced to 9
gittern	33	B2	reversed; 10 strings reduced to 6
hands stretching lute strings	40^v	I4^v	hands reversed; number of strings reduced
diagram of lute tuning	41^v	K3	basic outlines retained

Description	Location in Agricola (fol.)	Location in Virdung (fol.)	Major differences in Agricola version
4 fiddles (viols) with bows	46^v	B2	three fiddles added; reversed; position of bow changed; 9 strings reduced to a more credible 4
dulcimer	53^v	B2^v	hammers and shading lines on front reversed; centre bridge moved to one side
harp	54	B2^v	shading lines on front pillar reversed; shading lines on soundboard omitted and pitch names added; 23 strings increased to 26
psaltery	54^v	B2^v	simplified and pitch names added
4 small fiddles (rebecs)	55^v–56	B3	three fiddles added; reversed
trumpet marine	56	B3	reversed; position of bow changed
anvil with hammers	56^v	C2^v	reversed
small bells and bell	59	C2^v	reversed, except for (truncated) inscription on bell

APPENDIX 2
Pitches cited in the 1529 and 1545 editions of *Musica instrumentalis deudsch*, along with designations in letter-symbols

The 1529 edition gives four additional, lower notes for the bass crumhorn, expressed as large ornamental versions of **B**, **C**, **D** and **E**. Chromatic inflections of diatonic pitches are omitted here, except for forms of **B**♭ and **B**♮.

F	G	A	B [B♭]	H [B♮]	C	D	E	F	G	a
Ff	Γ			♮						
f	g	a	b	h ♮	c	d	e			

b [b♭]	h [b♮]	c	d	e	f	g	aa	bb [bb♭]
	♮						ā	b̄ [b̄♭]
	♮h						āa	b̄b

147

APPENDIX 3
Composite transcription of the fingering charts for recorders and related instruments on fols. 9–10 of the 1529 edition

Recorders sound an octave higher than the written notation.

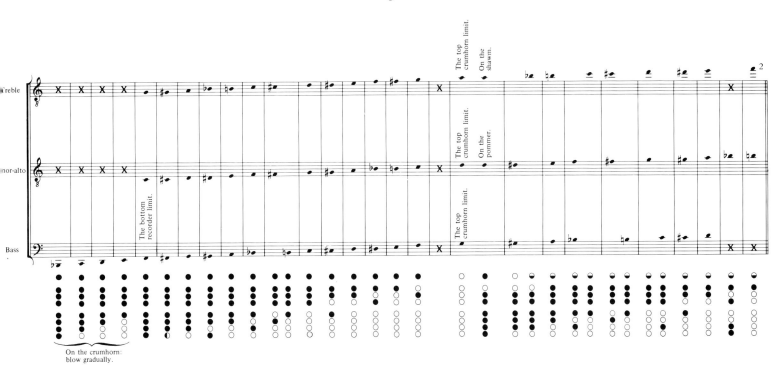

APPENDIX 4
Composite transcription of the fingering charts for Swiss flutes
on fols. 13ᵛ–14ᵛ of the 1529 edition

These flutes are evidently meant to sound an octave and a fourth higher than the
written notation.[3]

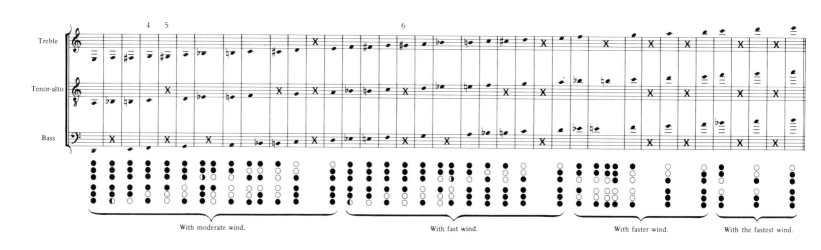

APPENDIX 5

Transcription of the fingering chart for the small recorder with four holes on fol. 15ᵛ of the 1529 edition and fol. 23 of the 1545 edition

This instrument evidently sounds at least two octaves higher than the written notation.[7]
The bottom row of circles indicates the bottom end of the instrument.

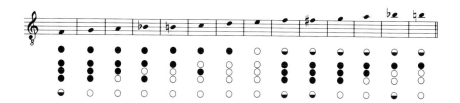

APPENDIX 6
Recto of the foldout, showing notes and rests in vocal notation and tablature, cited on fol. 25ᵛ of the 1529 edition

How the notes and rests are written in vocal notation, and how many beats [*schlege*] they signify; also how they are written and divided up in transcribing [into tablature].[8]

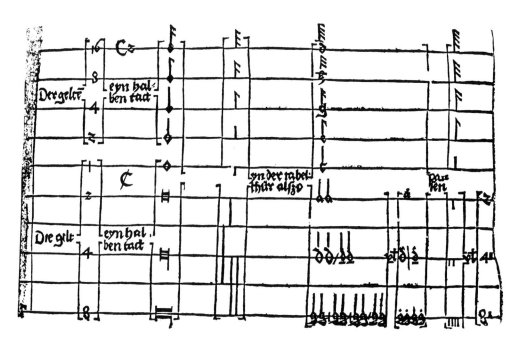

(*Upper left:* Of these, [the given number] equal a half-bar. *Lower left:* [Each of] these equals [the given number of] half-bars. *Across the middle:* Thus, in tablature. Rests. *Lower right:* The same as. The same as.)

APPENDIX 7
Verso of the foldout, showing a musical example in both vocal notation and tablature, cited on fol. 25ᵛ of the 1529 edition[9]

(*Top:* The method of composition. *Middle:* The method of organ tablature.)
[See Appendix 8 for a transcription of both types of notation in this example.]

APPENDIX 8

Transcription of both types of notation on the verso of the
foldout cited on fol. 25ᵛ of the 1529 edition

APPENDIX 9
Table derived from the diagram of the old lute tablature on fol. 36ᵛ of the 1529 edition[14]

Pitch	Symbol(s) for fingering(s)	Location(s) of fingering(s)
ee	[symbol]	g:9
dd#	[symbol]	g:8
dd	[symbol]	g:7
cc#	[symbol]	g:6
cc	[symbol]	g:5
bb♮	[symbol]	g:4 / d:9
bb♭	[symbol]	g:3 / d:8
aa	[symbol]	g:2 / d:7
g#	[symbol]	g:1 / d:6
g	[symbol]	g:0 / d:5
f#	[symbol]	d:4 / a:9
f	[symbol]	d:3 / a:8

Pitch	Symbol(s) for fingering(s)	Location(s) of fingering(s)
e	[symbol]	d:2 / a:7
d#	[symbol]	d:1 / a:6
d	[symbol]	d:0 / a:5 / F:9
c#	[symbol]	a:4 / F:8
c	[symbol]	a:3 / F:7
b♮	[symbol]	a:2 / F:6
b♭	[symbol]	a:1 / F:5
a	[symbol]	a:0 / F:4 / C:9
G#	[symbol]	F:3 / C:8
G	[symbol]	F:2 / C:7

Pitch	Symbol(s) for fingering(s)	Location(s) of fingering(s)
F#	[symbol] [15]	F:1 / C:6
F	[symbol]	F:0 / C:5
E	[symbol]	C:4 / Γ:9
D#	[symbol]	C:3 / Γ:8
D	[symbol] [16]	C:2 / Γ:7
C#	[symbol] [17] [18]	C:1 / Γ:6
C	[symbol]	C:0 / Γ:5
B♮	[symbol]	Γ:4
B♭	[symbol]	Γ:3
A	[symbol] [19]	Γ:2
G#	[symbol] [20]	Γ:1
Γ	[symbol]	Γ:0

APPENDIX 10

Table derived from the diagram of letters showing octaves in the
old lute tablature on fol. 37ᵛ of the 1529 edition

Pitch	Symbol(s) for fingering(s)	Pitch an octave lower	Symbol(s) for fingering(s)	Pitch	Symbol(s) for fingering(s)	Pitch an octave lower	Symbol(s) for fingering(s)
ee[21]	[22]	e		f		F	
dd#		d#		e		E	
dd		d		d#		D#	
cc#		c#		d		D	[24] [25]
cc		c		c#		C#	
bb♮		b♮		c		C	
bb♭		b♭		b♮		B♮	
aa		a		b♭		B♭	
g#	[23]	G#		a		A	[26]
g		G		G#		G#	
f#		F#		G		G	

156

APPENDIX 11

Recto of the foldout, showing a musical example in both mensural notation and tablature, cited on fol. 37[v] of the 1529 edition[27]

How each voice, by itself and separately, is changed and transcribed from the notes of vocal notation into letters.

(*Right column*: Vocal notation. Treble. Tablature. Tenor.)
[See Appendix 12 for a transcription of this example.]

APPENDIX 12

Transcription of the mensural notation and tablature on the
recto of the foldout cited on fol. 37[v] of the 1529 edition[28]

APPENDIX 13

Verso of the foldout, showing a musical example in new lute tablature, cited on fol. 37ᵛ of the 1529 edition

Here are all three voices written one above the other in lute tablature, as is proper.

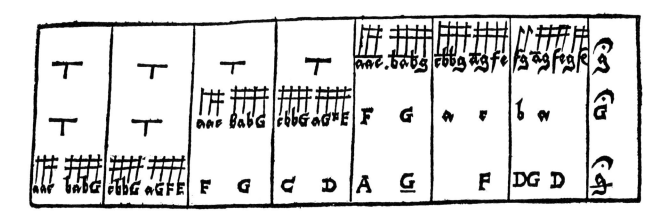

[See Appendix 14 for a transcription of this example.]

APPENDIX 14

Transcription of the tablature on the verso of the foldout cited
on fol. 37[v] of the 1529 edition[30]

APPENDIX 15

Table derived from the diagram of mensural notation and new
and old lute tablature on fol. 38 of the 1529 edition

Note value in mensural notation	Symbol(s) for note value and pitch in Agricola's new lute tablature	Symbol for rest in tablature notation	Symbol for note value and pitch in the old German lute tablature	Note value in mensural notation	Symbol(s) for note value and pitch in Agricola's new lute tablature	Symbol for rest in tablature notation	Symbol for note value and pitch in the old German lute tablature

Right-hand column of original diagram

Middle column of original diagram

Left-hand column of original diagram[39]

161

APPENDIX 16

Transcription of the setting of 'Ach Gott, vom Himmel sieh darein' in new lute tablature on fols. 38ᵛ–40 of the 1529 edition[43]

APPENDIX 17

The foldout, showing how to tune the strings of the lute by octaves, cited on fol. 42^v of the 1529 edition[52]

A fine diagram showing how to tune the strings correctly by octaves[53]

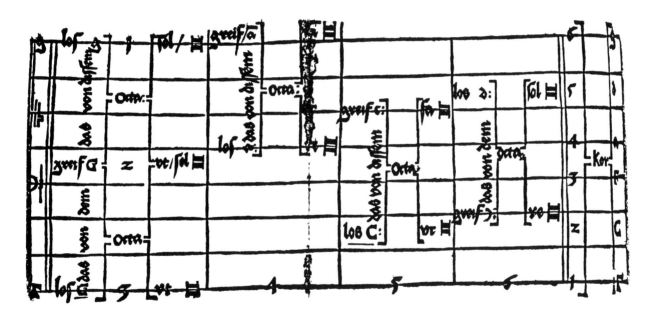

[See Appendix 18 for a table derived from (and incorporating the text presented in) this diagram.]

APPENDIX 18
Table derived from the diagram on the foldout cited on fol. 42ᵛ of the 1529 edition and the foldout cited on fol. 59 of the 1545 edition[54]

1 Tune the open **g** string (no. 6).
2 Tune the fingered **G** on the **F** string (no. 3) an octave lower than the **g** string.
3 Tune the open **G** string (no. 1) an octave lower than the fingered **G** on the **F** string.
4 Tune the open **a** string (no. 4) an octave lower than the fingered **ā** on the **g** string.
5 Tune the open **C** string (no. 2) an octave lower than the fingered **c** on the **a** string.
6 Tune the open **d** string (no. 5) an octave higher than the fingered **D** on the **C** string.

APPENDIX 19

Transcription of the musical example in both mensural notation
and tablature on fols. 52ᵛ and 53 of the 1529 edition[55]

APPENDIX 20
Composite transcription of the fingering charts for recorders and related instruments on fols. 20, 21 and 22 of the 1545 edition

Recorders sound an octave higher than the written notation.

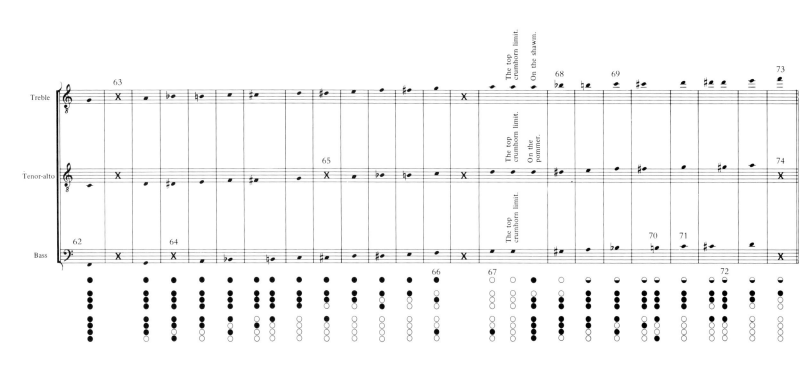

APPENDIX 21
Composite transcription of the fingering charts for Swiss flutes
on fols. 26ᵛ, 27ᵛ, 28 and 30ᵛ–31ᵛ of the 1545 edition

These flutes are evidently meant to sound an octave and a fifth higher than the
'irregular' notation and two octaves higher than the 'regular' notation.[75]

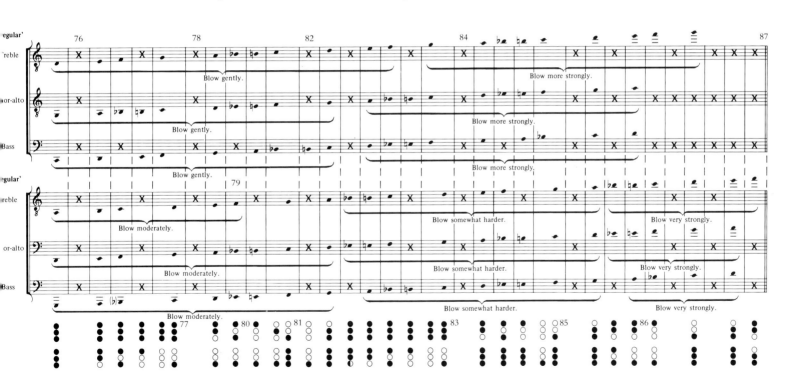

APPENDIX 22

Table of intervals derived from the instructions for measuring off the necks of the large Italian fiddle, the Polish fiddle and the small three-string, unfretted fiddle on fols. 41–42 and 49ᵛ of the 1545 edition

For purposes of comparison, only the pitches on the treble size are shown (the corresponding pitches on the other sizes are tuned the same as on the treble). All pitches shown here are set on the open **ā** string. The major third (**c̄#**) is not given for the large Italian fiddle.[88]

Pitch	Interval	Fraction of open string	Decimal equivalent
b̄ ♭	semitone	$\frac{243}{256}$	0.94922
b̄ ♮	whole-tone	$\frac{8}{9}$	0.88889
c̄	minor third	$\frac{27}{32}$	0.84375
c̄#	major third	$\frac{77}{96}$	0.80208
d̄	fourth	$\frac{3}{4}$	0.75000

APPENDIX 23

Table of intervals derived from the instructions for setting frets on the neck of the lute on fol. 53 of the 1545 edition

All pitches shown here are set on the open **g** string.[89]

Pitch	Interval	Fraction of open string	Decimal equivalent
g#	semitone	$\frac{77}{81}$	0.95062
ā	whole-tone	$\frac{8}{9}$	0.88889
b̄ ♭	minor third	$\frac{616}{729}$	0.84499
b̄ ♮	major third	$\frac{64}{81}$	0.79012
c̄	fourth	$\frac{3}{4}$	0.75000
c̄#	augmented fourth	$\frac{77}{108}$	0.71296
d̄	fifth	$\frac{2}{3}$	0.66667
ē	major sixth	$\frac{16}{27}$	0.59259

APPENDIX 24

The foldout, showing how to tune the strings of the lute by octaves, cited on fol. 59 of the 1545 edition[90]

A fine diagram showing how to tune the strings correctly by octaves

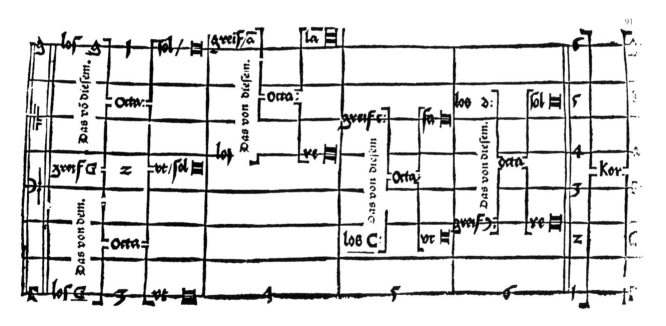

[See Appendix 18 for a table derived from (and incorporating the text presented in) this diagram.]

APPENDIX 25

Transcription of the foldout, showing the Pythagorean method of setting notes on the monochord, cited on fol. 63ᵛ of the 1545 edition

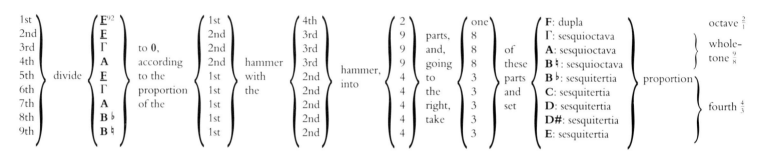

[See Appendix 26 for a table of intervals including those presented here.]

APPENDIX 26

Table of intervals derived from the instructions for setting notes on the monochord according to two methods: (1) as presented on fols. 61ᵛ–63 of the 1545 edition; and (2) as presented on the foldout cited on fol. 63ᵛ, and on fols. 64 and 64ᵛ of the 1545 edition[93]

Pitch	Method 1 Fraction of the string	Decimal equivalent	Method 2 Fraction of the string	Decimal equivalent	Pitch	Method 1 Fraction of the string	Decimal equivalent	Method 2 Fraction of the string	Decimal equivalent
E	$\frac{1}{1}$	1.00000	same		**G**	$\frac{4}{9}$	0.44444	same	
E#	not given		$\frac{243}{256}$	0.94922	**G#**	$\frac{512}{1215}$	0.42140	$\frac{27}{64}$	0.42188
Γ	$\frac{8}{9}$	0.88889	same		**a**	$\frac{32}{81}$	0.39506	same	
G#	not given		$\frac{27}{32}$	0.84375	**b ♭**	$\frac{3}{8}$	0.37500	same	
A	$\frac{64}{81}$	0.79012	same		**b ♮**	$\frac{256}{729}$	0.35117	same	
B ♭	$\frac{3}{4}$	0.75000	same		**c**	$\frac{1}{3}$	0.33333	same	
B ♮	$\frac{512}{729}$	0.70233	same		**c#**	$\frac{128}{405}$	0.31605	$\frac{81}{256}$	0.31641
C	$\frac{2}{3}$	0.66667	same		**d**	$\frac{8}{27}$	0.29630	same	
C#	$\frac{256}{405}$	0.63210	$\frac{81}{128}$	0.63281	**d#**	$\frac{1024}{3645}$	0.28093	$\frac{9}{32}$	0.28125
D	$\frac{16}{27}$	0.59259	same		**e**	$\frac{64}{243}$	0.26337	same	
D#	$\frac{2048}{3645}$	0.56187	$\frac{9}{16}$	0.56250	**f**	$\frac{1}{4}$	0.25000	same	
E	$\frac{128}{243}$	0.52675	same		**f#**	$\frac{32}{135}$	0.23704	$\frac{243}{1024}$	0.23730
F	$\frac{1}{2}$	0.50000	same		**g**	$\frac{2}{9}$	0.22222	same	
F#	$\frac{64}{135}$	0.47407	$\frac{243}{512}$	0.47461	**g#**	$\frac{256}{1215}$	0.21070	$\frac{27}{128}$	0.21094

Pitch	Method 1 Fraction of the string	Method 1 Decimal equivalent	Method 2 Fraction of the string	Method 2 Decimal equivalent	Pitch	Method 1 Fraction of the string	Method 1 Decimal equivalent	Method 2 Fraction of the string	Method 2 Decimal equivalent
aa	$\frac{16}{81}$	0.19753	same		**dd**	$\frac{4}{27}$	0.14815	same	
bb ♭	$\frac{3}{16}$	0.18750	same		**dd#**	$\frac{512}{3645}$	0.14047	$\frac{9}{64}$	0.14063
bb ♮	$\frac{128}{729}$	0.17558	same		**ee**	$\frac{32}{243}$	0.13169	same	
cc	$\frac{1}{6}$	0.16667	same		**ff**	$\frac{1}{8}$	0.12500	same	
cc#	$\frac{64}{405}$	0.15802	$\frac{81}{512}$	0.15820					

APPENDIX 27
Transcription of the foldout, showing the dimensions of organ pipes, cited on fol. 75^v of the 1545 edition[94]

Example

12 **G**, the octave, is 8 spans long, 2 spans wide.

11 **F#**,[95] the major seventh, is $8\frac{104}{243}$[96] spans long, $2\frac{26}{243}$ spans wide.

10 **F**, the minor seventh, is 9 spans long, $2\frac{1}{4}$ spans wide.

9 **E**, the major sixth, is $9\frac{13}{27}$ spans long, $2\frac{10}{27}$[97] spans wide.

8 **D#**, the minor sixth,[98] is $10\frac{1}{8}$[99] spans long, 2 and one-half plus $\frac{1}{32}$[100] spans wide.

7 **D**, the fifth, is 10 and one-half plus $\frac{1}{6}$[101] spans long, 2 and one-half plus $\frac{1}{6}$[102] spans wide.

6 **C**, the fourth, is 12 spans long, 3 spans wide.

5 **B♮**, the major third, is 12 and one-half plus $\frac{23}{162}$[103] spans long, $3\frac{13}{81}$ spans wide.

4 **B♭**, the minor third, is $13\frac{1}{2}$ spans long, $3\frac{3}{8}$ spans wide.

3 **A**, the whole-tone, is $14\frac{2}{9}$ spans long, $3\frac{5}{9}$ spans wide.

2 **G#**, the semitone, is $15\frac{3}{16}$ spans long, 3 and one-half plus $\frac{19}{64}$[104] spans wide.

1 **Γ**, the largest pipe, is 16 spans long, 4 spans wide.

Notes

Preface

1 The most extensive biographical study of Martin Agricola, still the standard work, is Heinz Funck, *Martin Agricola: Ein frühprotestantischer Schulmusiker* (Wolfenbüttel: Georg Kallmeyer Verlag, 1933). See also Bernhard Engelke, 'Agricola, Martinus', *Die Musik in Geschichte und Gegenwart*, ed. Friedrich Blume, vol. I (Kassel and Basel: Bärenreiter-Verlag, 1949–51), cols. 163–66.

2 Agricola's published writings on music are listed in François Lesure, ed., *Ecrits imprimés concernant la musique*, Repertoire international des sources musicales, BVI (Munich–Duisburg: G. Henle Verlag, 1971), vol. I, pp. 69–71. A list of publications in music, including Agricola's, that were issued from the press of Georg Rhau from 1528 to 1548 is given in Victor H. Mattfield, *Georg Rhaw's Publications for Vespers*, Musicological Studies, XI (Brooklyn, N.Y.: Institute of Mediaeval Music, 1966), pp. 351–53; this list is drawn from the study by Willi Woelbing, 'Der Drucker und Musikverleger Georg Rhaw' (Ph.D. diss., University of Berlin, 1922).

3 See Derq Howlett, 'A Translation of Three Treatises by Martin Agricola – *Musica choralis deudsch*, *Musica figuralis deudsch*, and *Von den Proporcionibus* – with Introduction, Transcriptions of the Music, and Commentary' (Ph.D. diss., The Ohio State University, 1979).

4 Funck, *Martin Agricola*, pp. 65–66.

5 The editions of this book are documented in Howard Mayer Brown, *Instrumental Music Printed before 1600: A Bibliography* (Cambridge, Mass.: Harvard University Press, 1967), pp. 27, 30–31, 40, 65–66 and 73; and in François Lesure, *Ecrits imprimés*, vol. I, pp. 70–71. Brown (p. 27) also lists a single copy of the work (found in the Sächsische Landes-bibliothek, Dresden) under the year 1528, which is derived from the dedication and is reported as 'the only date given in this edition'. From the configuration of the title page quoted by Brown, it seems most likely that this is a copy of the 1532 edition retaining the dedication (dated 1528) of the 1529 edition but lacking the page with the colophon indicating the date of printing. In fact, Lesure (p. 71) lists this among the surviving copies of the 1532 edition. Furthermore, Agricola's own references in his 1545 edition of *Musica instrumentalis deudsch* (fols. 3 and 29ᵛ) to the first edition of the work give its date clearly as 1529. The date of 1528 is perpetuated in the title of the only modern publication that presents the complete text of both the 1529 and the 1545 editions: Martin Agricola, *Musica instrumentalis deudsch, erste und vierte Ausgabe, Wittemberg 1528 und 1545, in neuer diplomatisch genauer, zum Teil fac-similierter Ausgabe*, Publikationen älterer praktischer und theoretischer Musikwerke, ed. Robert Eitner, vol. XX (Leipzig: Breitkopf & Härtel, 1896; reprint New York: Broude Brothers, 1966). Hereafter referred to as the 'Eitner edition', this is not a facsimile reproduction of the original sources, but rather a diplomatic presentation of the text with completely redrawn illustrations (containing numerous errors). The 1529 edition is presented in a true facsimile (although lacking the diagrams printed on the three foldout sheets) along with three other treatises of the author·in Martin Agricola, *Musica figuralis deudsch (1532): im Anhang, Musica instrumentalis deudsch (1529), Musica choralis deudsch (1533), Rudimenta musices (1539)* (Hildesheim, New York: Georg Olms Verlag, 1969). A translation and comparison of the 1529 edition with other treatises of the sixteenth and seventeenth centuries is found in William W. Hollaway, 'Martin Agricola's *Musica instrumentalis deudsch*: A Translation' (Ph.D. diss., North Texas State University, 1972); unfortunately, this translation is not trustworthy, and all of the illustrative material is copied from the Eitner edition, not from an original copy of the treatise. My own translation, into English verse, of sections of both editions dealing with woodwind instruments includes true facsimiles of all pages in question: William E. Hettrick, 'Martin Agricola's Poetic Discussion of the Recorder and Other Woodwind Instruments: A Translation with Commentary', part 1: 1529, *The American Recorder* 21, no. 3 (November 1980): 103–13; part 2: 1545,

ibid., vol. 23, no. 4 (November 1982): 139–46, and vol. 24, no. 2 (May 1983): 51–60; both parts were reprinted in *The Recorder and Music Magazine* 8, no. 4 (December 1984): 127–29, no. 5 (March 1985): 139–48, no. 6 (June 1985): 171–79, and no. 7 (September 1985): 202–12.

6 The most recent facsimile edition of this work is Sebastian Virdung, *Musica getutscht, 1511*, ed. Klaus Wolfgang Niemöller, Documenta musicologica, series 1, vol. XXXI (Kassel: Bärenreiter Verlag, 1970). Major studies include: Franz Krautwurst, 'Bemerkungen zu Sebastian Virdungs "Musica getutscht" (1511)', *Festschrift Bruno Stäblein zum 70. Geburtstag*, ed. Martin Ruhnke (Kassel: Bärenreiter Verlag, 1967), pp. 143–56; Edwin M. Ripin, 'A Reevaluation of Virdung's *Musica getutscht*', *Journal of the American Musicological Society* 29 (1976): 189–223; Gerhard Stradner, *Spielpraxis und Instrumentarium um 1500, dargestellt an Sebastian Virdungs 'Musica getutscht' (Basel 1511)* (Vienna: Verband der wissenschaftlichen Gesellschaften Österreichs, 1983); Beth Alice Baehr Bullard, 'Musical Instruments in the Early Sixteenth Century: A Translation and Historical Study of Sebastian Virdung's *Musica getutscht* (Basel, 1511)' (Ph.D. diss., University of Pennsylvania, 1987); and Beth Bullard, *Musica getutscht: A Treatise on Musical Instruments (1511) by Sebastian Virdung* (Cambridge University Press, 1993).

7 *Musica getutscht* was, in fact, an excerpt from a larger work written in German poetry, which Virdung mentions in his dedication (sig. A2).

8 Textual and illustrative material repeated from the 1529 edition is cited here in individual notes in the translation of the 1545 edition. This includes the presentation of the small recorder with four holes (1529, fols. 15–15ᵛ; 1545, fols. 22ᵛ–23), the discussion of brass instruments (1529, fol. 16; 1545, fol. 28ᵛ) and a number of diagrams and illustrations.

9 This section (specifically fols. 7–8, 9–9ᵛ and 11ᵛ) is the source of much of the admonitory text set to music by Paul Hindemith in his Plöner Musiktag cantata of 1932 entitled *Mahnung an die Jugend, sich der Musik zu befleissigen* (Mainz: B. Schott's Söhne, 1932). Hindemith took the rest of his text from Agricola's 1529 edition, fols. 8 and 30ᵛ–31.

10 Lesure, *Écrits imprimés*, vol. I, pp. 70–71.

11 According to Eitner's final statement on p. 287, this edition was based on four copies of the treatise. They are not identified, however, and it is not even clear whether this statement refers exclusively to the 1529 edition.

12 This copy is the source of the facsimile edition of the 1529 edition published by Georg Olms Verlag in 1969 (see above, note 5).

13 A microfilm of the Wolfenbüttel copy was made available through the Deutsches Musikgeschichtliches Archiv in Kassel.

14 Hettrick, 'Martin Agricola's Poetic Discussion'.

15 Ibid., vol. 21, no. 3 (November 1980): 110.

The 1529 edition

1 *Ein kurtz deudsche Musica* (Wittenberg: Georg Rhau, 1528).

2 Both *Jörg* and *Jorg*, found later in the dedication, are forms of the name *Georg*.

3 The *rüspfeiff*, mentioned here in the text and illustrated on fol. 11ᵛ (where the name is spelt *rüspfeyff*), is the same instrument as the *ruszpfeif* pictured by Virdung on fol. B4 of his *Musica getutscht*. The illustrations in these two sources depict it as a small fipple-flute with a straight (Virdung) or slightly tapered (Agricola) profile running from the squared-off mouthpiece to the point where the integral, slightly flaring bell begins. The absence of shading lines in the pictures (otherwise used to show rounded objects in both books) may indicate that the upper portion of the instrument's body has a square or rectangular shape in cross section, and that the four fingerholes – no thumbhole is indicated – are cut into one of the flat sides. Considerable speculation exists in the organological literature concerning both the physical characteristics and the name of this instrument. One source of confusion is the similar 'small recorder with four holes', of which Agricola gives a description, illustration and fingering chart in both of his editions (1529, fols. 15–15ᵛ; 1545, fols. 22ᵛ–23ᵛ); another is the French flageolet, first described and pictured by Marin Mersenne in his *Harmonie universelle* (Paris, 1636). The name *rüspfeiff* (*ruszpfeif*) itself has proved enigmatic to many writers, especially those who have drawn a connexion between it and the term *Rauschpfeife*, which was generally used in the sixteenth century to denote wind instruments with sounding reeds. Other attempts to identify the instrument through etymology have led to the

following interpretations of its name: 'reed pipe' (i.e., made of cane), 'noisy pipe', 'Russian pipe' and 'black pipe'. All of this information is discussed and documented in my recent article on the subject, which also proposes a theory that the instrument's name indicates elmwood as the material of construction; see William E. Hettrick, 'Identifying and Defining the *Ruszpfeif*: Some Observations and Etymological Theories', *Journal of the American Musical Instrument Society* 17 (1991): 53–68.

4   This word, *ungegriffen* in the original, is given incorrectly as *angegriffen* in the Eitner edition, p. 10.

5   *In margin*: ● ⊙ 1 2 3 4 5 6 7 8 ♯. ●. [The duplicated filled-in circle at the end is evidently meant to refer to the next line in the text.]

6   *In margin*: Bass **Ff**.

7   *In margin*: Tenor **C**, treble **G** [like the corresponding reference in the text, this pitch designation is given incorrectly as **g**].

8   Given incorrectly as **g** in the original.

9   *In margin*: ⊙.

10 *In margin*: Bass **G**, tenor **d**, treble **aa**.

11 *In margin*: ♯ 4 3 2 1.

12 This description of the fingering for the second-highest note on recorders does not tally completely with any of the three fingering charts. In the chart for the bass the note in question is **c**, but the given fingering does not include the opened second hole, as indicated in the text. The corresponding notes in the other two charts (**g** for the tenor-alto and **dd** for the treble) have the indicated fingering, but these are the third notes down from the top.

13 *In margin*: Bass **c** [like the corresponding reference in the text, this is given incorrectly as **C**], tenor **g**, treble **dd**.

14 Given incorrectly as **C** in the original.

15 *In margin*: **C** ℞, **d** ℞, **f** ℞, **g** ℞. [This note missing in the A and F copies.]

16 The original reading of this line is: *Das du die pfeiff nicht blest wie die Pauren*. The Eitner edition (p. 13) substitutes *nicht* for the first *die*, thus erroneously producing two appearances of the word ·*nicht*.

17 *In margin*: Concerning the crumhorns. [This note missing in the A and F copies.]

18 *In margin*: The old tablature for wind instruments. [This note missing in the A and F copies.]

19 Agricola is probably referring here to Sebastian Virdung, whose discussion of recorders in *Musica getutsch* (sig. M3ᵛ–O4) presents, for every pitch on the bass, tenor and treble sizes, both a fingering and a single symbol based on a number. Virdung calls the latter symbols, collectively, tablature.

20 *In margin*: Chapter 9. [In fact, it is in chapter 11 that the tablature for fiddles and other monophonic instruments is presented.]

21 That is, referring to pitches by their letter-names, as opposed to using numbers to symbolise the pitches in question.

22 *In margin*: Such as all kinds of wind instruments and fiddles. [This note missing in the A and F copies.]

23 All three of Agricola's charts give fingerings for recorders and crumhorns, while the tenor-alto chart includes the pommer and the treble chart the shawm. No mention is made of cornetts and bagpipes, however.

24 These woodcut illustrations of four recorders were clearly modelled on those printed in Virdung's *Musica getutsch* (see Appendix 1). In keeping with the practice of having two instruments of the same size play the alto and tenor parts in four-part ensembles, Virdung's illustrated group of four recorders was intended to show only the three sizes discussed in his text: the bass pictured on top, two examples of the tenor given in the middle, and the treble illustrated at the bottom. Virdung's artist depicted the three sizes approximately in correct proportion to each other, but made the two middle-sized instruments with slightly different lengths. Agricola's artist, in turn, increased this discrepancy, but decreased the differences in length between adjacent sizes, thereby destroying the proportions and giving the erroneous impression of four distinct sizes.

25 Given incorrectly as **C** in the H copy. Although Agricola indicates above (fol. 5) that the hands may be placed on the recorder in either order, the illustrations at the bottoms of these three fingering charts show the right hand at the top and the left hand at the bottom.

26 In the A, F and N copies (and the Eitner edition) the rectangular fingering charts for the tenor-alto and the treble are transposed, so that the treble chart is printed on fol. 9ᵛ and the tenor-alto chart is on fol. 10. The marginal material (including the horizontal illustration of

the recorder at the bottom and the vertical caption at the side), however, is correctly positioned. The present edition places the charts in the correct order, following the H copy.

27 Given incorrectly as *Bij.*

28 Agricola makes clear the distinction between this instrument (*Krumphorn*) and the crumhorns (*Kromphörner, odder Pfeiffen*) shown above: although *horn* might refer to any wind instrument, *pfeiff* would not be used for a lip-vibrated one. In the H copy the woodcuts of the *Platerspiel* and the *Krumphorn* are printed upside-down.

29 The H copy has *Zigenhorn.*

30 *In margin*: 1 2 3 4 5 6 ●.

31 *In margin*: From **D** [this is given incorrectly as **D**] to **D**.

32 *In margin*: From **E** to **d**.

33 *In margin*: **e f g aa**.

34 *In margin*: **bb ♭ cc dd**.

35 As in the case of the illustration of the four recorders, the flutes identified here as the alto and tenor should be shown as the same size. Virdung depicts only a single transverse flute.

36 Here Agricola returns to his policy (stated for recorders on fol. 5) of allowing either arrangement of the two hands on vertical woodwind instruments.

37 This name, which is linked with the French *clairon* by Sibyl Marcuse (*Musical Instruments: A Comprehensive Dictionary* (New York: W. W. Norton & Company, Inc., 1975), pp. 104–05), was used by both Virdung and Agricola for a trumpet with a narrow bore that would probably favour higher pitches.

38 All four of the illustrations on fol. 16ᵛ were derived from Virdung (see Appendix 1), whose depictions of the clareta and the tower trumpet are transposed in the A, F and N copies of Agricola's 1529 edition (this is the version shown in the Eitner edition). The H copy agrees with Virdung in showing the clareta more credibly as the refined version of the military trumpet with its folded shape, while the tower trumpet is the instrument with the more archaic S-shape. The erroneous transposition was retained in the 1545 edition (fol. 29), however, and because that is evidently the version preferred by Agricola (if only by default), it is the one shown here.

39 *In margin*: Chapter 3.

40 In the diagram on fol. 19ᵛ, the horizontal lines (in this case reading the diagram with the book turned 90° so that its gutter is at the top of the page) are drawn in by hand in the original copies, mostly through the letters and syllables, and are meant to be seen as lines of the musical staff. The '4 finals' referred to are D, E, F and G, the finals of the four authentic melodic modes.

41 As in the previous chart, the horizontal lines here (perpendicular to the gutter of the book) are drawn in by hand in the original copies.

42 Although printed separately, the ♮ and **h** in the following line were probably intended to constitute a double letter (♮**h**) indicating **bb♮**. Note that they are represented by a single **ħ** in the tablature notation that follows. The other examples, below, of both ♮ and **h** (or **H**) – as given in small, large or underlined letters – seem to be meant as alternate designations of the same pitch.

43 *In margin*: Treble.

44 *In margin*: Tenor.

45 The second symbol in the following line, **G**, should either be underlined or expressed as **Γ**; in this context, the latter seems preferable.

46 *In margin*: Bass.

47 Note that the following series of underlined letters goes only through **e** (indicating the same pitch as **E**) and therefore does not include symbols corresponding to **F** and **G** in the series above. The diagram of the organ keyboard on fol. 26ᵛ shows that the pitches in question would be indicated as capital letters in both series.

48 The time signature under *Pausen* in this diagram is given as **₵2** in the H and N copies.

49 Note values shown in the examples of ligatures will be identified here in the notes by means of the following abbreviations: M (maxima), L (long), B (breve) and S (semibreve). The note values in the first example are LL, LBL, LBB, LB, B.

50 BB, BBB, BBL, L.

51 BBB, BB, BBL, B.

52 SS, SS, SSL, SSB, B.

53 LBL, SSBBB, LBL, LBBBBBBBB, SSBBBBBBBB, L. The first two notes in the fourth ligature in this example (LB) are written as an ascending oblique with no stem descending from the beginning. Opinion is divided as to whether the first note should be read as a breve

or a long, but the weight of evidence seems to support the latter interpretation. See Willi Apel, *The Notation of Polyphonic Music 900–1600* (Cambridge, Mass.: The Mediaeval Academy of America, 1953), pp. 90–91, note 1.

54 LL, BL, SSL, BBBL, SSL.

55 BB, BBB, SSB, SSB, SSBBB, SS. The descending stem between the second and third notes of the third ligature (SB) seems to have no significance, since it would have to apply to the second note (making it a long), which, however, is already identified as a semibreve by the ascending stem at the beginning of the first note.

56 SSB, BBB, SSBB, SSB, SS, SS.

57 MBBBMBBMBBBMBBM.

58 In the fifteenth and early sixteenth centuries, the word *Clavicymbal* (in its various forms stemming from the Latin *clavicimbalum*) generally denoted a stringed, quilled keyboard instrument, usually in harpsichord shape; see Marcuse, *Musical Instruments*, pp. 85 and 115. Virdung's virginal (sig. B) and *Clavicimbalum* (sig. Bᵛ) both have the same shape, and Agricola's artist seems to have used the latter as the basis of his illustrations of both instruments (fols. 27 and 27ᵛ; see Appendix 1).

59 The name 'symphony' was applied to the hurdy-gurdy (organistrum) in the late Middle Ages; see Curt Sachs, *Real-Lexikon der Musikinstrumente* rev. edn (New York: Dover Publications, 1964), p. 367.

60 Two pitch symbols shown here do not agree with the corresponding examples on fol. 20ᵛ. The lowest key is identified with a double letter here in both methods of notating the bottom octave, while on fol. 20ᵛ the symbol in the underlined series is **f**. Also, the symbol for the **bb**♮ in the top octave is overlined here in both methods (**h̄** and **♮̄**), while the latter example would seem to require only a double lower-case letter.

61 This woodcut is positioned upside-down in the H and N copies.

62 The illustration of this instrument on fol. 33 shows that it is the mandola (mandora), a small lute with a sickle-shaped pegbox.

63 *In margin*: Chapter 8. [The number is missing in the A and F copies. Chapter 8 deals only with the first type of large fiddles.]

64 *In margin*: Chapter 14. [Of the instruments mentioned, only the xylophone is treated in chapter 14.]

65 Although Agricola does not name the blind lute player, this statement surely refers to Virdung's report in *Musica getutscht* (sig. K3ᵛ) of having heard that German lute tablature was invented by 'a blind man born in Nuremberg and buried in Munich, who was called Master Conrad of Nuremberg', a reference to the organist and lutenist Conrad Paumann (ca. 1410–73). Willi Apel (*The Notation of Polyphonic Music*, pp. 72 and 74) confuses the matter considerably by attributing the identification of Paumann directly to Agricola and not mentioning Virdung at all in this context, and then by refuting Agricola's supposedly unequivocal identification on the grounds that 'a blind man is not very likely to have invented a notational system' – the very argument that Agricola himself uses to ridicule the system in question. See also Christoph Wolff, 'Paumann, Conrad', *The New Grove Dictionary of Music and Musicians*, ed. Stanley Sadie (London: Macmillan Publishers Ltd., 1980), vol. XIV, pp. 308–09.

66 Starting at this point, six lines in the text are identified, respectively, with the numbers 1, 2, 3, 4, 5 and 6 in a vertical column in the margin. Additionally, each of the six numbers corresponds with a letter, and the resulting six letters, also positioned in a vertical column, spell *Musica*.

67 The initial letters of the six lines referred to here correspond to the word *Musica* presented vertically in the margin. The fifth line of this acrostic begins with the letter Z (*Zu*), an equivalent of C in German. The sixth line begins with a puzzling I (*Ich*) in the A and F copies and the Eitner edition, while the H and N copies have the expected A (*Auch*) here. The present translation reflects the latter, obviously correct reading.

68 *In margin*: Something from book 2 of *Fasti*. [In this section of his work, Ovid recounts the story of Arion and the dolphin.]

69 In most accounts of this story the animal is cited as a dolphin.

70 *In margin*: Music.

71 Agricola includes both **B** and **H** in his total.

72 Similarly, both **b** and **h** are counted.

73 Again, both **bb** and **hh** are counted.

74 The alternate methods of showing the doubled letters, both small and large, are given above on fol. 20ᵛ.

75 By the time of Agricola's writing, lute music notated in German tablature had been printed in Virdung, *Musica getutscht* (sig. M2ᵛ–M3: 'O hailige, onbeflecte', now acknowledged as unplayable); Arnolt Schlick, *Tabulaturen etlicher lobgesang und lidlein uff die orgeln und lauten*

(Mainz, 1512); and in Hans Judenkunig's two books, *Utilis & compendiaria introductio* (Vienna, n.d.) and *Ain schone kunstliche underweisung* (Vienna, 1523). For further information on the contents of these publications, see Brown, *Instrumental Music Printed before 1600*, pp. 20–27.

76 In this diagram the horizontal and vertical lines show graphically the number of strands of gut to be used, respectively, for the frets and the courses of strings. The former consist of two strands each, while the latter are double courses except for the highest pitch, which is single. The principle of German lute tablature – as discussed in Apel, *The Notation of Polyphonic Music*, pp. 72–81 – is that every intersection of string course and fret is given a separate symbol. Based originally on a five-string lute, this system begins with the open strings **C**, **F**, **a**, **d** and **g**, which are numbered consecutively from **1** to **5** (as shown at the bottom in Agricola's diagram). Then, starting with the first fret (shown at the top in the diagram), twenty-three letters of the alphabet (beginning with capital A and then going on with lower-case letters, with j and w omitted and u and v united into one character) are deployed, moving across the fingerboard in the same order of strings and then going on to each next fret in turn. Before the alphabet begins again at the intersection of the **C** string and the sixth fret, two extra-alphabetical symbols – corresponding to the Latin abbreviations for *et* and *con*, respectively – are used for the last two intersections (**d**:5 and **g**:5). The open and stopped positions along the lowest string (Γ) are marked with symbols derived from those used for the adjacent **C** string, but with a line above: thus, **1̄** is taken from **1**, **Ā** from **A**, **f̄** from **f** and so on. Similarly, the letters of the second alphabet (for the five highest strings) are distinguished from those of the first by lines above the characters; but since the same method is used to show the Γ-string derivations from the **C** string, a dot is placed over the line over the **A** and the **f** in the second octave so that these symbols will not be confused with symbols already employed for the first two frets on the Γ string. Agricola's diagram contains several symbols that must be commented on in addition. The symbol for **B** ♭ (Γ:3) is simply a lower-case **l** with a line through it, not a **t**, as the Eitner edition seems to render it. The designation of the pitch **G#** (**F**:3) is incorrectly given as **C#**. The designation of the pitch **F** (**C**:5) is incorrectly given as **f**

(followed by *fa*, indicating that it is a semitone above **E**). The symbol for **D** (Γ:7) is given as **f̿f̿**, while **f̄** would have sufficed. Finally, the dot above the symbol for **aa** (**d**:7) simply belongs to the letter **i** and has no additional significance.

77 Agricola's method here is to use the letter-names of the pitches as the symbols for the positions on the fingerboard. In spite of the apparent ease of reading afforded by this method, it seems not to have been adopted by other musicians, perhaps because different ways of playing the same pitch (e.g., the pitch **C** as **C**:0 or as Γ:5) are not distinguished, and other types of idiomatic tablature were available. Note that this diagram shows no difference in the symbols used for **B** ♮ (Γ:4) and **b** ♮ (**F**:6 and **a**:2), rendering all three positions with the same double-character symbol. The symbol for **b̄** ♮ (**g**:4) likewise contains two characters.

78 Here Agricola tunes the Γ string down to **E**, thus gaining this pitch at the bottom of the register. Note that the designation of **F#** (**E**:1) is incorrectly given as **E**. Unlike the diagram on fol. 34, here the symbols for **B** ♮ (**E**:6) and **b** ♮ (**F**:6 and **a**:2) look different, the former being larger than the latter two, as would be expected. Again, all three symbols contain two (alternate?) characters, as does the symbol for **b̄** ♮ (**g**:4).

79 Incorrectly given as *xxxvi*.

80 *In margin*: **1̄** Γ.

81 *In margin*: **1 C**.

82 *In margin*: **2 F**.

83 *In margin*: **3 a**.

84 *In margin*: **4 d**.

85 *In margin*: **5 g**.

86 Given as **D** in the original because it is capitalised as the first letter of the line.

87 *In margin*: **g 5**.

88 All of the tuning procedures given here involving stopped strings on lutes and fiddles require, of course, that the frets be set correctly beforehand.

89 This is given incorrectly as **a** in the original.

90 In the column containing syllables at about the centre of the diagram, the diagonal lines link those of the same hexachord. Thus, starting at the

bottom, Γ and **C** are *ut* and *fa*, respectively, in the G hexachord; **C** and **F** are *ut* and *fa* in the C hexachord; and so on. The diagram lacks a (perhaps unnecessary) line at the top of the column showing that **d** and **g** are *re* and *sol* in the C hexachord.

91 The characteristics of Agricola's first type of large fiddles, as presented here, allow these instruments to be identified as members of the viola da gamba family. He does not illustrate this first type, nor does he indicate the playing positions of any of his bowed string instruments.

92 The tuning of the treble is **F**, **a**, **d**, **g** and **c̄**.

93 The tuning of the tenor(-alto) is **C**, **F**, **a**, **d** and **g**.

94 The tuning of the bass is **G̲**, **C**, **F**, **a**, **d** and **g**.

95 This procedure requires that the pitch of the highest string (**c̄**) first be established.

96 The numbers are given in the original as 1, 2, 4 and 5.

97 This pitch is given incorrectly as **Ḡ** in the A and F copies (the overline seems to have been drawn in by hand) and the Eitner edition. The H and N copies have the correct reading given here.

98 As in all of Agricola's diagrams of fingerboards, the pitches of the open strings of each instrument are shown here in a horizontal row at the bottom, while the pitches of the successive stopped positions are shown beginning at the top.

99 The pictures of four-string fiddles on fol. 46ᵛ are evidently meant to illustrate this second type. Although four different sizes of instruments are shown, Agricola's text makes it clear that the alto and tenor (together referred to variously as 'tenor' and 'tenor-alto') are tuned the same. The tuning patterns of all these sizes – involving fourths and major thirds – relate this second type of fiddles, like the first type, to the viola da gamba family. Ian Woodfield (*The Early History of the Viol* (Cambridge University Press, 1984), pp. 100–01) has commented that Agricola's pictures on fol. 46ᵛ were derived from Virdung's woodcut (sig. B2) illustrating the *gross Geigen* (see Appendix 1) with the retention of significant characteristics such as the 'bizarre' design with 'huge waists and awkwardly projecting shoulders' and the absence of arched bridges (attributed to an oversight on Agricola's part), but also with important changes: the reduction of the number of strings and pegs from nine to four and the concomitant narrowing of the fingerboard.

100 The tuning of the treble is **G**, **c**, **f** and **ā**.

101 The tuning of the tenor(-alto) is **C**, **F**, **a** and **d**.

102 The tuning of the bass is **G̲**, **C**, **F** and **a**.

103 *In margin*: **ā**.

104 Procedures 3 and 4 require that the string being tuned also be stopped, a very awkward method that is much harder to execute than tuning an open string.

105 Agricola could also have instructed that the open **d** in the tenor-alto be tuned in unison to the fingered **d** on the **c** string in the treble.

106 The line under the **G** seems to have been drawn in by hand in all of the copies consulted.

107 Note that the amount of space in which four frets are shown for the bass and alto-tenor in this schematic diagram accommodates five frets for the treble. A pitch (**d̄**) is indicated for this fifth fret, however, only in connexion with the highest string, for which pitches representing the sixth and seventh frets (**d̄#** and **ē**) are also given. Otherwise, for the two lowest strings (**G** and **c**), pitches for only four frets are indicated; and only three frets' worth of pitches are given for the **f** string – just enough to fill in the major third between the **f** and **ā** strings.

108 The characteristics of Agricola's third type of fiddles, as presented here in his text and the illustrations on fols. 51ᵛ and 52, seem to be related to the viola da braccio family.

109 *In margin*: **ā**.

110 The tuning of the treble is **G**, **d** and **ā**.

111 The H and N copies have **d** here. The correct line above the letter is present in the A and F copies, probably drawn in by hand.

112 The tuning of the tenor(-alto) is **C**, **G** and **d**.

113 The tuning of the bass is **F̲**, **C** and **G**.

114 This pitch is indicated by a larger capital letter (with no underline) in the original.

115 The A and F copies and the Eitner edition have an incorrect *Erste* here; the correct *Eylfft* is given in the H and N copies.

116 The pictures shown on fols. 51ᵛ and 52 are evidently meant to illustrate the instruments described on fols. 49–50ᵛ. Note that they are depicted – as announced in the preceding caption – with frets attached, which Agricola recommends be used by beginners. Again, four different sizes are illustrated, although Agricola's text makes it clear that the alto and

tenor have the same tuning. Like the woodcuts on fol. 46ᵛ, these pictures seem to be derived from Virdung's *gross Geigen* (sig. B2), having the instruments' shape and absence of arched bridges in common with that earlier source.

117 This folio is incorrectly numbered *liiij* in the A and N copies.

118 The following pitches are shown on the harp, reading from the highest to the lowest: c̄, b̄♮/b̄♭, ā, ḡ, f̄, ē, d̄, c̄, b♮/b♭, a, g, f, e, d, c, b♮/b♭, a, G, F, E, D (the letter indicating this pitch is incorrectly underlined), C, B♮/B♭, A, **G** and **F**.

119 The following pitches are shown on the psaltery, reading from the highest to the lowest: b̄♭, ā, ḡ, f̄, ē, d̄, c̄, b♮/b♭, ā, g, f, e, d, c, b♮ /b♭, a, G, F, E, D, C, B♮/B♭, A, **G** and **F**.

120 The two examples that Agricola gives for this type make it clear that the strings he refers to here as 'courses' (a word he otherwise uses in connexion with the lute, dulcimer, harp and psaltery) are single, as is the case with all the bowed string instruments he presents.

121 Agricola's illustrations of these instruments on fols. 55ᵛ and 56 show that they are rebecs.

122 Note that the identifications of the bass and tenor of the rebec family are transposed in the illustrations on fol. 56.

123 This point marks the end of the text on fol. 57 in the F, H and N copies. The arrangement presented here is that found in the A copy and also the Eitner edition.

124 This caption faces the gutter of the book in the F, H and N copies.

125 Given incorrectly as *Viij* in the Eitner edition.

126 This caption faces the illustration in the F, H and N copies.

127 The following pitches are shown on the xylophone, reading from the highest to the lowest: f̄, ē, d̄, c̄, b♮, b̄♭, ā, g, f, e, d, c, b♮, b♭, a, G, F, E, D, C, B♮, B♭, A, **G** (the letter indicating this pitch is not underlined) and **F**.

The 1545 edition

1 *In margin*: Introduction.

2 *In margin*: The first reason for the publication.

3 *In margin*: The great council of Magdeburg: a commendation.

4 *In margin*: The second reason for the publication. [This marginal note is set lower on the page than the text to which it refers.]

5 This is a reference to the 1529 edition of *Musica instrumentalis deudsch*.

6 *In margin*: In the year 1529. [This marginal note is set lower on the page than the text to which it refers.]

7 *In margin*: Who could count the individual virtues of this most agreeable discipline?

8 *In margin*: Apoc. 4, Isa. 6.

9 The instrumental pieces referred to here are probably those printed posthumously in Agricola's *Duo libri musices* (Wittenberg: Georg Rhau's Successors, 1561).

10 Here Agricola describes his attackers as monastic; although he does not specifically say so, he is surely referring to the Roman Catholic clergy, probably those of the Magdeburg cathedral, who remained loyal to Rome until the cathedral was closed by the Protestant city council in 1546. See Funck, *Martin Agricola*, p. 79.

11 This 'you' and the one that follows (both given as *du*, the form used later in the preface to refer to the scorner) seem to indicate Georg Rhau, although he is otherwise addressed as *ihr*.

12 *In margin*: Solomon, Moses, David, Elisha, Josh. 6, Job 21, Eph. 5, Col. 3, Num. 10 etc.

13 *In margin*: Dedication of the very little book.

14 This 'you' (*ihr*) refers to Rhau, not the scorner (*du*) cited immediately above.

15 *In margin*: Lady Music [abbreviated as *F.M.*].

16 Agricola also dedicated his *Ein kurtz deudsche Musica* (1528; 2nd edn, 1529; 3rd edn as *Musica choralis deudsch*, 1533) and *Musica instrumentalis deudsch* (1529) to Rhau.

17 *In margin*: Epilogue.

18 This is abbreviated as *E.W.A.* (*Ewr Williger Anhänger?*).

19 *In margin*: MUSICA. [This is presented vertically as a six-letter acrostic, corresponding to the initial letters of the six lines of text.]

20 *In margin*: MARTINUS. [This is presented vertically as an eight-letter acrostic, corresponding to the initial letters of the eight lines of text.]

21 *In margin*: SORE. [This is presented vertically as a four-letter acrostic, corresponding to the initial lettters of the four lines of text.]

22 *In margin*: The goal [*Scopus*, given incorrectly as *Seopus*] of individual musical instruments.

23 This may be a reference to the practice of sending choirboys (*Currende*) out on the streets to sing for money.

24 *In margin*: Lady Music [abbreviated as *F.M.*].

25 *In margin*: The nature of Music.

26 *In margin*: Lady Music [abbreviated as *F.M.*].

27 *In margin*: From childhood, this most noble lady alone was most pleasing to me.

28 *In margin*: Penitence out of season [i.e., too late].

29 *In margin*: Who does not understand how to play keeps away from contests on the fields [i.e., the Campus Martius]. [Horace, *Ars poetica*, 379.]

30 *In margin*: Amplification.

31 *In margin*: 1 Tim. 6: [10]. The love of money is the root of all evil.

32 *In margin*: I speak as an experienced man.

33 *In margin*: Who seeks to gain wickedly loses badly.

34 *In margin*: The story of a certain soldier.

35 *In margin*: Lady Music [abbreviated as *F.M.*].

36 *In margin*: About whom see [Aulus] Gellius, book 18 of the *Noctes Atticae*. [The citation is in error: it is in book 16, chapter 19, of this work that the story of Arion is presented.]

37 *In margin*: In the year 1544.

38 The nobleman referred to here has not been identified.

39 *In margin*: Giving thanks to Music.

40 *In margin*: An exhortation to the children of the rich.

41 The following quotation and its author have not been identified.

42 *In margin*: Conclusion.

43 *In margin*: Of all the different liberal arts, music is the oldest and most pleasing.

44 *In margin*: A suggestion to the poor.

45 *In margin*: If you do not want to do this, then you may stand guard.

46 *In margin*: Amplification.

47 *In margin*: A just censure of papist priests.

48 *In margin*: Papists do not employ the true sacrament, but rather the simple element of bread and wine.

49 *In margin*: Dr Martin Luther [abbreviated as *D.M.L.*].

50 *In margin*: Licentiate Nicolaus Glossenus [abbreviated as *L.N.G.*], minister at St Ulrich's and superintendent of the school at Magdeburg.

51 A vigorous opponent of the Roman Catholic clergy in Magdeburg, especially at the cathedral, Glossenus became pastor at the Church of St Ulrich and superintendent of its school in 1542. See Friedrich Wilhelm Hoffmann, *Geschichte der Stadt Magdeburg*, vol. II (Magdeburg: Verlag von Emil Baensch, 1847), p. 178.

52 *In margin*: Drink ye all of this etc.

53 *In margin*: Irony.

54 *In margin*: On the day of Corpus Christi, as they call it.

55 Pope Paul III (reg. 1534–49).

56 This point marks the end of a section unique in the poetic text of both editions of Agricola's treatise, in that three lines, all with the same end rhymes, are placed together. It is questionable whether this was an oversight on Agricola's part, or whether he intended to give special emphasis through this device.

57 Charles V, Holy Roman emperor (reg. 1519–56).

58 *In margin*: In the year 1545.

59 Martin Luther, *Wider das Bapstum zu Rom vom Teuffel gestifft* (Wittenberg, 1545); see *D. Martin Luthers Werke*, vol. LIV (Weimar: Hermann Böhlaus Nachfolger, 1928).

60 *In margin*: The book of Exodus.

61 *In margin*: Precaution.

62 *In margin*: Every sprout that God did not plant will be rooted up [Matt. 15: 13].

63 *In margin*: We ought to obey God rather than men [Acts 5: 29].

64 *In margin*: One now sees more through the fingers than through spectacles. Gifts appease men and gods etc. Let everyone be on guard. [These three sentences are in different languages: the first German, the second Latin and the third Low German.]

65 *In margin*: A general exhortation to boys.

66 This famous statement in Plato's *Republic*, book 5, was transmitted by Boethius, *De consolatione philosophiae*, 1, 4.

67 *In margin*: In praise of learned men.

68 *In margin*: Epilogue to the preface.

69 In the 1529 edition, Agricola indicates that the hands may be in either order (fol. 5); but here he specifically advocates that the right hand be

uppermost (the opposite of modern practice). This coincides with the illustrations of recorders and hands shown in conjunction with the three fingering charts in both editions of the treatise.

70 Agricola refers to the diagram on fol. 17ᵛ, which has vertical columns of figures on both left and right sides, except for the number 1 at the bottom, given once for both columns, which is placed at the centre between the two duplicate bottom fingerholes.

71 Although chapter 1 begins on fol. 7, this is the first running head that indicates the chapter number. The illustration on this page is repeated from the 1529 edition, fol. 8ᵛ.

72 The relative positions of the duplicate bottom holes, one shown open and the other plugged, indicate a playing position with the left hand above the right hand. This arrangement conflicts with the one advocated on fol. 16.

73 *In margin*: Treble ●, **G**, all holes closed.

74 An incorrect 5 is added to this fingering in the Eitner edition, p. 155.

75 The numbers 2 and 6, both incorrect, are added to this fingering in the Eitner edition, p. 155.

76 *In margin*: Treble ○, all holes opened.

77 In fact, the fingering diagram for the treble is not presented until three pages later (fol. 20), the tenor diagram two pages after that (fol. 21), and the one for the bass two pages later (fol. 22).

78 The illustration is repeated from the 1529 edition, fol. 10ᵛ.

79 *In margin*: The diatonic category of music exists when a fourth is made to sound the same as two whole-tones and one minor semitone.

80 This illustration, which belongs with the diagram on fol. 20, is repeated from the 1529 edition, fol. 10.

81 This illustration is repeated from the 1529 edition, fol. 9ᵛ.

82 This illustration is repeated from the 1529 edition, fol. 9.

83 This page has the same text as that found on fol. 15 of the 1529 edition, although it has been reset, with some changes in spelling and in the layout of the heading.

84 The text on this page is the same as that found on fol. 15ᵛ of the 1529 edition, except that it has been reset with some changes in spelling. The fingering chart here is identical to the one on fol. 15ᵛ of the 1529 edition.

85 This illustration is repeated from the 1529 edition, fol. 15ᵛ.

86 The remaining illustrations on this page are repeated from the 1529 edition, fol. 11. On Agricola's distinction between the names of the crumhorns and the curved horn, see above, 1529 edition, note 28.

87 In fact, Agricola's fingering charts contain no reference to the cornett and bagpipe.

88 The arrangement of the hands on the flute shown in the illustration on fol. 25 (the opposite of modern practice) coincides with that indicated for the recorder on fol. 16. Fingered in this way, of course, the flute would extend out to the left of the player's head.

89 The Eitner edition gives this running head as *Der Instrument. Musica* ('Of musical instruments').

90 The illustrations of the alto, tenor and bass flutes are repeated from the 1529 edition (fol. 13), kept in the same order from left to right, but turned upside-down (therefore showing a reversal of the order of the wood blocks for the individual pictures). The illustration of the treble is new (note that the shading is opposite to that shown on the other three flutes; perhaps this indicates that the picture in question was copied from the 1529 edition in the same way that many of the illustrations in that edition seem to have been copied from Virdung's treatise).

91 See fol. 42ᵛ.

92 The Tremulant, a device found on several organs of the early sixteenth century, produced regular fluctuations of wind pressure (and therefore pitch) by means of a flap that opened a hole cut into the wind trunk. An early use of this device is documented on the organ built in 1496 in Sorau (near Agricola's home city of Schwiebus and probably the origin of his original surname, Sore), and he may have been familiar with this instrument. See Christhard Mahrenholz, *Die Orgelregister: Ihre Geschichte und ihr Bau*, 2nd edn, reprint (Kassel: Bärenreiter-Verlag, 1968), pp. 278–79.

93 *In margin*: If you know something it is of no use unless another person knows it also.

94 The twelve lines that follow here and take up the rest of the page are the same as those found on fol. 16 of the 1529 edition, except that they are reset with some changes in spelling. This material seems misplaced here, as it interrupts the discussion of transverse flutes, which resumes on fol. 29ᵛ.

95 See above, 1529 edition, note 37.

96 This promise, made first in the 1529 edition, was still unfulfilled in 1545.
97 The illustration of the four brass instruments on fol. 29 is repeated from the 1529 edition, fol. 16ᵛ, along with the incorrect matching of names and pictures of the clareta and the tower trumpet, as found in most of the consulted copies of that edition. The perpetuation of this error (in spite of its correction in the H copy of the 1529 edition), the disruptive placement of the entire repeated text on brass instruments (see above, note 94), and the telling repetition of the author's admission of ignorance (see above, note 96) all suggest an oversight on Agricola's part or, at the least, his lack of control over the order and contents of his book, whose composition he probably was unable to supervise personally because of the distance between Magdeburg and Wittenberg.
98 *In margin*: In the year 1529.
99 *In margin*: Just as in song, so also in musical instruments, a transposition of the melody can be made.
100 *In margin*: The best foundation for this category of flutes.
101 *In margin*: The same application for the fusa and semifusa.
102 The illustration of the bagpipe on fol. 33 is repeated from the 1529 edition, fol. 11ᵛ.
103 Matt. 10: 8.
104 *In margin*: Phil. 2: [21].
105 *In margin*: The application of the tongue to the playing of woodwind instruments.
106 This refers to the double-tonguing of consecutive semiminims or fusas, as illustrated in the notation on fols. 34 and 34ᵛ.
107 Agricola's example shows that consecutive minims are to be played by single-tonguing, semiminims by either single- or double-tonguing, and fusas by double-tonguing exclusively. Alternating the consonants *d* and *r* for the latter is only one of the several methods recommended by Sylvestro Ganassi in his *Opera intitulata Fontegara* (Venice, 1535), chapter 7.
108 Here Agricola uses tablature notation to show a group of eight fusas, the first being articulated with the syllable *tel* and the succeeding seven with the syllable *lel*. These are the notes that make up the indicated half-measure. The final syllable, *le*, has no corresponding note. The method of articulation shown in this example is not found in Ganassi, ibid., where the letter *l* is used only in alternation with *r*.

109 *In margin*: Let any of these figures have its own particular length. Let it be extended according to the requirement of its own value.
110 *In margin*: The imperfect and diminished breve can also be bowed as the length of an entire measure.
111 *In margin*: As is treated in chapter 11 of the previous Instrumental [Music].
112 Each of the following three lines of letters begins with a number, in the order: 3, 2, 1.
113 The (correct) line under the second letter in the example, perhaps drawn in by hand in the Augsburg copy as shown here, is missing in the Wolfenbüttel copy and the Eitner edition.
114 These 'large Italian fiddles' can be identified as members of the viola da gamba family. They correspond generally in range and number of strings to Agricola's second type of 'large fiddles' in the 1529 edition (fols. 46ᵛ–48ᵛ), although the bass now has an added bottom string tuned to **E**, and the treble may accommodate a higher register, either through the addition of a top string tuned to **d̄** or through an alternate tuning of the four strings a fourth higher.
115 This heading refers to the diagram on fol. 37. Note that the diagram does not show a complete chromatic scale (lacking **d#** and **g#**). In addition, if the fourth fret is meant to be placed a semitone above the third, the pitch played by the fourth finger on the **ā** string should be **c̄#**, not **d̄** as given.
116 The pitches of the open strings – **c**, **e**, **ā** and **dd** (i.e., **d̄**) – are given in the right-hand column. This tuning, a fourth higher than the one given on fol. 37, places the treble an octave higher than the tenor–alto. Note that a complete chromatic scale is not shown, lacking **g#** and **c̄#**.
117 Agricola's word, *Testudo*, was normally applied to the lute in the sixteenth century. Here it would appear to have a more general meaning.
118 This diagram does not show a continuous chromatic scale, lacking **C#**, **G#** and **c#**. Also, as in the case of the treble diagram, the fourth fret is probably meant to be a semitone above the third, and therefore the fourth finger on the **d** string will play **f#**, not **g** as given.
119 Again Agricola uses a word (*Cithara*) that was sometimes interpreted as 'lute' in the sixteenth century.

120 Here the pitches **F#** and **G#** on the **F** string are not identified, nor is a fourth fret (necessary for **C#** and **F#**) shown.

121 Here the **F** string appears to serve the purpose only of providing the open-string pitch, since **F#** is lacking in the diagram, which also omits **G#**. Note that **B♮** (the print is defective here, lacking the ascending line) is indicated for the fourth fret on the Γ string, while on the **a** string the pitch shown for the same fret is **d** (it should be **c#**).

122 The illustration of four fiddles on this page is repeated exactly from fol. 46ᵛ of the 1529 edition, where it is evidently meant to illustrate the second type of large fiddles, which have frets and only four strings (see the 1529 edition, note 99). Here the pictures seem to refer to the large Italian fiddles described on fols. 36ᵛ–39, although the bass size is clearly indicated as having five strings.

123 *In margin*: The dividers are the unique master of the arts.

124 *In margin*: The marks of the beginning of the measuring: treble **ā**, tenor **d**, bass **a**.

125 *In margin*: What is said is true because by itself it signifies nothing, but it makes other numbers signify more.

126 Sibyl Marcuse (*Musical Instruments*, p. 418) cites Agricola's reference to the *Polnische Geige* and adds two more citations, also from the sixteenth century. The conjectural nature of her comment on the instrument's origin seems unnecessary in view of Agricola's definite statement that they were 'common in Poland'. These fiddles are probably related to the viola da braccio family.

127 This line reads *Dann eine mit den fingern weich* in the original; the word *den* is omitted in the Eitner edition.

128 *In margin*: Nothing is so difficult that it cannot be attained through continual practice.

129 The diagrams in question are those that begin on fol. 46.

130 The instruments referred to here are the large Italian fiddles, not the Polish ones.

131 All three intervals in this diagram are expressed as lower intervals in the original, referring to the position of the open string being tuned as compared to the higher pitch used as a model.

132 Both this and the preceding example show the same pitches for the open strings, and the difference lies in the methods used to obtain the pitches. Here the player is evidently expected to be able to tune the open strings solely by ear, according to the stated intervals.

133 *In margin*: A humorous discourse.

134 Agricola refers here specifically to his agrarian origins.

135 Literally, 'Workmen handle their own tools'. Horace, *Epistulae*, 2, 1, 116.

136 A sixth stopped position would be necessary to provide the pitches for a complete chromatic scale from **G** to **d̄**: **c#** (**G**:6) and **g#** (**d**:6).

137 Likewise, a sixth stopped position would be necessary to provide the chromatic pitches **F#** (**C**:6) and **c#** (**G**:6). Note also that **C#** (**C**:1) is not identified.

138 Again, a sixth stopped position would provide the chromatic pitches **C#** (Γ:6) and **G#** (**D**:6). Note also that **G#** (Γ:1) is not identified, and that the open **F** string seems to function only to provide that pitch, since **F#** is not given.

139 Presumably this method would allow the bass to have only three strings, tuned **F**, **C** and **G**.

140 Agricola's small fiddles are rebecs. The illustrations of the treble and alto are repeated from the 1529 edition, fol. 55ᵛ. Likewise, the pictures – presented here on fol. 48ᵛ – of the tenor and bass (now correctly identified; see the 1529 edition, note 122) and the trumpet marine (again not mentioned in the text) are repeated from the 1529 edition, fol. 56.

141 The Eitner edition gives an incorrect **0** here.

142 The open **F** is in fact two octaves below the fingered **f**.

143 *In margin*: Note.

144 *In margin*: The ornamentation of the organ is the best.

145 *In margin*: Preparing the neck of the lute.

146 *In margin*: The beginning of the measuring.

147 *In margin*: The end of the measuring.

148 *In margin*: Note.

149 Agricola evidently refers here to the practice of stretching a stopped string that sounds the upper pitch of a perfect fifth in order to increase the size of the interval.

150 This passage is correctly interpreted by Mark Lindley (*Lutes, Viols and Temperaments* (Cambridge University Press, 1984), p. 22) as indicating

equal temperament. Lindley does not, however, relate the fact that Agricola goes on to ridicule this practice.

151 Lindley (ibid.) quotes this passage incompletely, implying that Agricola states that all frets in equal temperament are placed the distance of a minor semitone apart.

152 This tablature differs from the one shown on fol. 34 of the 1529 edition in that the earlier one makes no graphic distinction between two different positions producing the same pitch (e.g., **G** played as either **C**:7 or **F**:2), while the present tablature shows duplicated pitches by either of two methods: by means of the pertinent letter both with and without underlining (e.g., **G** for **C**:7 and **G** for **F**:2 – although it should be noted that the use of the underline is reserved here only for pitches played on the higher frets of the lower three strings and is in direct opposition to the system of pitch designation employed elsewhere in this treatise); or by means of different graphic forms of the letter in question. These two methods are further illustrated in the diagram on fol. 55.

153 The diagram on fol. 56 clearly shows seven courses, of which the lowest six are double and the highest is single, thus totalling thirteen strings.

154 The diagram on fol. 56 gives two symbols for each intersection of string (course) and fret: the higher one follows Agricola's new tablature as presented on fols. 54ᵛ and 55, while the lower one represents the old tablature as announced. These old-tablature symbols coincide with those shown on fol. 33ᵛ of the 1529 edition (the symbol for **d**:6, producing **g#**, in the Augsburg copy is **d̄**, as given here; in the Wolfenbüttel copy and the Eitner edition it lacks the line above the letter). In spite of the listing on fol. 55ᵛ of pitches obtainable by stopping the **Ff** string, this diagram shows only the open **Ff**, probably because the old tablature lacks symbols for the added intersections.

155 This heading and the text that follows on fols. 56ᵛ–57ᵛ and 58ᵛ–59 are very similar to the presentation of the same subject in the 1529 edition, fols. 40ᵛ–41 and 42–42ᵛ. The illustration shown here in the left margin is repeated (showing some deterioration of the wood block) from fol. 40ᵛ of the 1529 edition.

156 In the 1529 edition (fol. 40ᵛ) it is the thumb that is designated for this purpose.

157 This running head is in error; it should read *Von der Lauten* ('Concerning the lute').

158 *In margin*: **Γ**, **1̄**.

159 The original gives this pitch incorrectly as **G**.

160 *In margin*: **C**, **1**.

161 *In margin*: **F**, **2**.

162 *In margin*: **a**, **3**.

163 *In margin*: **d**, **4**.

164 *In margin*: **g**, **5**.

165 The original gives this pitch incorrectly as **G**.

166 This diagram is repeated from the 1529 edition, fol. 41ᵛ.

167 The original gives this pitch incorrectly as **G**.

168 The original gives this pitch incorrectly as **d̄**.

169 The illustrations of both the lute and the gittern on fol. 60 are repeated from the 1529 edition, fol. 33.

170 *In margin*: A description of the monochord.

171 A span is the distance from the tip of the thumb to the tip of the little finger, commonly taken as 9 in. or 23 cm. Thus 6 spans measure 54 in. or 138 cm.

172 Thus 4.5 in. or 11.5 cm.

173 *In margin*: The brief measuring of the monochord.

174 The original gives this pitch incorrectly as **F**.

175 By analogy with the symbol used above to mark the bridge end of fiddle and lute strings, this figure is to be interpreted as the numeral zero.

176 *In margin*: The hidden or invisible line.

177 The line under this letter seems to be drawn in by hand in the Augsburg copy.

178 The line under this letter seems to be drawn in by hand in the Augsburg copy.

179 This running head is in error; it should read *Von dem Monochord* ('Concerning the monochord').

180 *In margin*: The measuring of the semitones.

181 All chromatic pitches in the three-octave span from **F̱** to **ff** are accounted for except **F̱#** and **G̱#**.

182 The line under this letter seems to be drawn in by hand in the Augsburg copy.

183 *In margin:* The proof of the measuring.

184 This illustration is repeated from the 1529 edition, fol. 56ᵛ.

185 This continues the numbering begun with 1–9 in the foldout cited on fol. 63ᵛ.

186 *In margin:* The measuring of the remaining semitones.

187 *In margin:* $\frac{4}{3}$.

188 This letter is not underlined in the original.

189 *In margin:* Each octave will be apportioned according to the requirement of dupla proportion, $\frac{2}{1}$.

190 This folio number is given incorrectly in the original as 64.

191 *In margin:* According to the declarations of Berno [of Reichenau] and Guido [of Arezzo] etc.

192 *In margin:* Macrobius, book 2 of the *Somnium Scipionis.* Also Boethius etc.

193 *In margin:* The sounds of the 4 hammers: 1. whole-tone, 2. fourth, 3. fifth, 4. octave. [As explained in the text that follows, the intervals in question were heard between the pitches produced by four hammers taken two at a time in various combinations.]

194 *In margin:* The discovery of speculative music.

195 *In margin:* $\frac{12}{6}$, octave.

196 *In margin:* $\frac{9}{6}$, fifth.

197 *In margin:* $\frac{12}{9}$, fourth.

198 *In margin:* $\frac{9}{8}$, whole-tone.

199 *In margin:* Pythagoras was the first discoverer of speculative music.

200 Agricola refers here to the diagram on fol. 68.

201 Macrobius, *Commentarium in somnium Scipionis,* 2, 1. Agricola's quotation, which takes up the rest of fol. 67ᵛ, differs slightly from the corresponding text as presented in *Macrobii Ambrosii Theodosii opera quae supersunt,* ed. Ludovicus Janus, vol. I (Quedlinburg and Leipzig: Godofredus Bassius, 1848), p. 134. The transcription of this passage in the Eitner edition (p. 254) is incorrect in the penultimate line, where *sidum* should read *fidum.* The translation given here is based on that found in Macrobius, *Commentary on the Dream of Scipio,* trans. William Harris Stahl (New York: Columbia University Press, 1952), p. 187. Copyright © (1952) Columbia University Press, New York. Used by permission.

202 This illustration is repeated from the 1529 edition, fol. 58.

203 This illustration is repeated from the 1529 edition, fol. 58ᵛ.

204 *In margin:* The definition of proportion.

205 *In margin:* An excuse for the abridged definition of proportion.

206 *In margin:* In the year 1532.

207 *Musica figuralis deudsch* (Wittenberg: Georg Rhau, 1532), see chapter 12. The division of proportions is treated specifically in Agricola's *Von den Proporcionibus* (Wittenberg: Georg Rhau, 1532), chapter 1. Note that in these two books the proportions in question have to do with note values. In the present discussion proportions refer to pitch intervals.

208 *In margin:* The adding of proportions.

209 *In margin:* The lower is called the denominator, the upper the numerator.

210 *In margin:* $\frac{24}{16}$.

211 *In margin:* $\frac{32}{24}$.

212 *In margin:* Fifth.

213 *In margin:* Fourth.

214 *In margin:* $\frac{12}{6}$, dupla.

215 *In margin:* The subtracting of a proportion from a proportion.

216 The procedure described on fols. 72 and 72ᵛ is an example of Euclid's algorithm for finding the greatest common divisor.

217 *In margin:* $\frac{16}{12}$, fourth.

218 The proportions presented here follow the Pythagorean system.

219 *In margin:* The theoretical proportions of 44 musical intervals.

220 This is also known as the 'diatonic' semitone.

221 This is also known as the 'chromatic' semitone.

222 Note that the diminished fifth (no. 9) is a larger interval than the augmented fourth (no. 8).

223 *In margin:* 1st octave.

224 The second number of this proportion is given incorrectly in the Augsburg copy (and the Eitner edition, p. 265) as 5012. In the Wolfenbüttel copy the incorrect zero is removed, but a space remains where it was.

225 The second numbers of this and the preceding proportion are transposed in the original, leading to the incorrect reading of no. 21 as 256:2048 and no. 22 as 729:729.

226 This proportion could have been reduced to 1:3.

227 *In margin:* 2nd octave.

228 This proportion could have been reduced to 2:9.

229 This proportion could have been reduced to 16:81.

230 This proportion could have been reduced to 128:729.

231 This proportion could have been reduced to 1:6.

232 This proportion could have been reduced to 4:27.

233 This proportion could have been reduced to 32:243.

234 *In margin*: 3rd octave.

235 *In margin*: 4th octave.

236 The proportions corresponding to these last four intervals are all incorrect in the original, reading as follows: no. 41, 72:1; no. 42, 32:3; no. 43, 12:1; and no. 44, 16:1. The mistakes in the last three are the result of transposition of the two numbers in each proportion, while the first combines transposition with an incorrect number.

237 *In margin*: The rule of three, or the golden rule, is a manifestation of secret matters.

238 See above, note 171.

239 *In margin*: The length.

240 *In margin*: The width. And in the same manner with respect to the rest.

241 In the original, *spannen* ('spans') is placed incorrectly under this number.

242 The Eitner edition (p. 269) gives this number incorrectly as $2\frac{1}{3}$.

243 Luke 16: 2 and a reference to the parable of the talents, Matt. 25: 14–30.

244 The announced diagram begins on fol. 77ᵛ. Both of the illustrations that follow on this page, the group of small bells and the larger bell, are repeated from the 1529 edition, fol. 59.

245 The proportions presented in the diagram on fols. 77ᵛ–78 follow the Pythagorean system. The two pages of the diagram are presented here as they appear in the Augsburg copy. They are reversed (with the indications of the octaves placed in the outside margins) in the Wolfenbüttel copy and the Eitner edition. The editorial fraction given here in square brackets following each indication of weight represents the proportion of the weight of the bell in question to that of the largest bell, **F** (16 lb.).

246 A loth (*lot*) is equal to $\frac{1}{2}$ oz. (thus $\frac{1}{32}$ lb.).

247 The numerator of this fraction is given incorrectly in the original as 129.

248 A quentin is equal to $\frac{1}{4}$ loth (thus $\frac{1}{8}$ oz. or $\frac{1}{128}$ lb.).

249 The denominator of this fraction is given incorrectly in the original as 72.

250 The numerator of this fraction is given incorrectly in the original as 196.

251 The numerator of this fraction is given incorrectly in the original as 247.

252 This illustration is repeated from the 1529 edition, fol. 54. The following pitches are shown on the harp, reading from the highest to the lowest: c̄, b̄♮/b̄♭, ā, ḡ, f̄, ē, d̄, c̄, b♮/b♭, ā, g, f, e, d, c, b♮/ b♭, a, G, F, E, D (as in the 1529 edition, the letter indicating this pitch is incorrectly underlined), C, B♮/B♭, A, **G** and **F**.

253 This illustration is repeated from the 1529 edition, fol. 54ᵛ. The following pitches are shown on the psaltery, reading from the highest to the lowest: b̄♭, ā, ḡ, f̄, ē, d̄, c̄, b♮/b♭, ā, g, f, e, d, c, b♮/ b♭, a, G, F, E, D, C, B♮/B♭, A, **G** and **F**.

254 This illustration is repeated from the 1529 edition, fol. 59ᵛ. The following pitches are shown on the xylophone, reading from the highest to the lowest: f̄, ē, d̄, c̄, b♮, b̄♭, ā, g, f, e, d, c, b♮, b♭, a, G, F, E, D, C, B♮, B♭, A, **G** (as in the 1529 edition, the letter indicating this pitch is not underlined), and **F**.

255 This illustration is repeated from the 1529 edition, fol. 53ᵛ.

256 *In margin*: The conclusion of the little work.

257 *In margin*: An excuse.

258 *In margin*: The study of music is difficult without a teacher.

259 *In margin*: Lady Music [abbreviated as *F.M.*].

260 *In margin*: No day without an outline. [The origin of this proverb is given by Pliny the Elder in his *Historia naturalis*, book 35: the Greek painter Apelles strictly observed the practice of not letting a day go by without tracing an outline of something.] More fully about these things elsewhere.

261 *In margin*: A request.

262 *In margin*: Luke 10: [7], 1 Tim. 5: [18].

263 *In margin*: 1 Cor. 9: [9]. [This quotation is also found in 1 Tim. 5: 18.]

264 This is abbreviated as *M.A.*

265 This is abbreviated as *E.W.* See above, note 18.

266 This verb, *nachgan*, has *ihm* (singular) as its object; it should be the plural *ihn* (*ihnen*).

267 Agricola ends with a reference to the same instrumental pieces mentioned in the preface. See above, note 9.

Appendices

1 Virdung's woodcut of the clavicymbalum appears to have been used by Agricola's artist as a model for his illustrations of both the clavicimbalum and the virginal. Virdung's virginal (sig. B) has a different keyboard and shading lines on the underside of the lid.

2 The context of the fingering chart makes it clear that **ff** is intended here, not **ff#**; yet the indicated fingering would produce the latter pitch. The correct fingering for **ff** in the treble should be the same as for **b♭** in the tenor-alto. (Agricola repeats the same fingering for **ff** in the treble in his 1545 edition. See Appendix 20, note 73.)

3 The indicated interval of transposition between the notated and the actual (nominal) pitches of the flute family is corroborated by information on the three flute sizes given by Michael Praetorius, *Syntagma musicum*, vol. II: *De organographia* (Wolfenbüttel, 1619), p. 22, and *Theatrum instrumentorum* (Wolfenbüttel, 1620), plate 9. See also Howard Mayer Brown, 'Notes (and Transposing Notes) on the Transverse Flute in the Early Sixteenth Century', *Journal of the American Musical Instrument Society* 12 (1986): 22.

4 The fingering for **G** in the treble indicates holes 1 and 2 opened (i.e., the fingering for **G#**).

5 Notated as **F#** in the treble, with the fingering given as having only hole 2 opened (i.e., the fingering for **G**).

6 Notated as **f#** in the treble, with the fingering given as having only hole 2 opened (i.e., the fingering for **g**).

7 Note that both **f** and **f#** are given the same fingering on the chart. This instrument appears to be the same as the *gar klein Plockflötlein* described by Praetorius (*De organographia*, p. 34) and illustrated as the highest member of the recorder family (*Theatrum instrumentorum*, plate 9). Both instruments have a thumbhole and three fingerholes. Praetorius shows his model as being two octaves above his tenor recorder (which has the same nominal pitch as Agricola's tenor-alto), and thus its lowest written pitch, assuming the application of Agricola's technique of half-closing the bottom end of the pipe after all the other holes are closed, would be two octaves above Agricola's **c**. Without being more specific, Praetorius says that the instrument's range is 'almost two octaves'. Agricola's fingering chart shows a somewhat smaller range of an octave and an augmented fourth starting on written **F**. If both instruments were of the same size, the notation of Agricola's fingering chart would be two octaves and a fifth below the actual pitch (and therefore one octave and a fifth below the normal recorder notation). Of course there is no evidence to preclude the possibility that Agricola's instrument was nominally a fifth lower than Praetorius's, in which case the interval between the written notation and the actual pitch would be two octaves.

8 The left-hand vertical column in the diagram, shaded over in this facsimile, contains clefs that give pitch identification to the horizontal lines, as follows (reading from the bottom to the top): 1st line, Γ; 4th line, 𝄢; 6th line, 𝄡; 8th line, **g**; 10th line, **dd**.

9 The type of notation shown at the bottom, with letters used for all parts but the highest, which is notated on a staff, is usually designated as 'old German organ tablature'.

10 These two minims are represented by a single semibreve **G** in the tablature. In bar 3 the note is a defective breve in the mensural notation, but the pitch is clearly **F**, as opposed to the **G** given in the Eitner edition. In bar 4 the **D** is indicated as a minim in the tablature.

11 This and the next two **b**'s in the top part are not indicated as flatted in the tablature. The following two **b**'s, however, appear with slashed (extra) descending stems, indicating chromatic inflexion.

12 The dots after this note and the one directly below it in the bass part appear to be missing in the tablature notation.

13 This and the following **f** are indicated as **f#** in the tablature by means of slashed descending stems.

14 Agricola's diagram on fol. 36ᵛ includes symbols for fingerings requiring the eighth and ninth frets; they represent extensions of the diagram on fol. 33ᵛ, which goes up only to the seventh fret.

15 This is given as **Ā** on fol. 33ᵛ.

16 This is given as **f̄f̄** on fol. 33ᵛ.

17 This is given as **A** on fol. 33ᵛ.

18 This is given as **ĀA** on fol. 33ᵛ.

19 This is given as **f̃** on fol. 33ᵛ.

20 This is given as **Ā** on fol. 33ᵛ.

21 All eight of these double letters have an unnecessary line above the first letter in the diagram.

22 The line above this symbol coincides with the top horizontal line framing the diagram.

23 This is given incorrectly as **d** in the diagram.

24 This is given as **a** on fol. 36ᵛ.

25 This is given as **A̅A̅** on fol. 33ᵛ and as **a̿a** on fol. 36ᵛ.

26 This is given as **a̅** on fol. 36ᵛ.

27 Two of Agricola's foldouts in the 1529 edition have material printed on both recto and verso sides: the one cited on fol. 25ᵛ and the present one. In both cases the most logical order of presentation begins with the side marked with the reference symbol in question (asterisks and/or trefoils) as the recto. In the present example the sides identified here (editorially) as recto and verso are bound into the A copy in reverse order.

28 The two versions differ in four places (bars 1, 3, 4 and 5) in which the mensural notation has a dotted minim, while the tablature has a minim and a semiminim, with both notes of the same pitch. The mensural notation is expressed here by means of broken tie signs.

29 This is given as **g** in the tablature.

30 This is the same as the example presented on the recto of the foldout cited on fol. 37ᵛ, but with simplifications in the tenor (bars 5–7) and bass (bars 4 and 6). The note values in the treble (bar 8), tenor (bar 5 on) and bass (bar 3 on) are indicated by the relative positions of the letters.

31 The Eitner edition gives this pitch incorrectly as **F**.

32 These four fusas are incorrectly given as semiminims in the tablature.

33 This is given as **g** in the tablature.

34 This symbol indicates **g**:10.

35 Both of these symbols, of course, mean the same thing. In Agricola's tablature, note values of a breve and larger are expressed as an appropriate number of semibreves.

36 Here Agricola does not retain the method of indicating a breve by means of a dot, as shown above on fol. 21 and the recto of the foldout cited on fol. 25ᵛ of the 1529 edition (see Appendix 6).

37 A vertical line indicating one semibreve is incorrectly printed above this symbol in the diagram.

38 Both of these symbols (each given twice) indicate the same pitch.

39 The time signatures placed in the left margin (**C** , **₵** and **C 2**) indicate the metrical contexts in which the given note values are found.

40 Again, both symbols indicate the same pitch.

41 Both of these symbols (one given as the first and fourth items, and the other as the second and third) indicate the same pitch.

42 Both of these symbols (each given four times) indicate the same pitch.

43 This contrapuntal setting of the indicated chorale, more extensive than the other musical examples, is presumably of Agricola's own composition.

44 Agricola's choice of **a̅** for this semibreve is probably a mistake, since the note could only be held for a minim's worth and would have to be fingered as **d**:7 in order to allow the **c̄** and **b̅** ♭ above it to be played as **g**:5 and **g**:3. Agricola must have intended to write the note an octave lower, **a**, which – as an open string – is much easier to play and is in the same octave as the rest of the line presenting the cantus firmus. The present transcription reflects Agricola's presumed intention.

45 This semiminim **F** seems to be an example of Agricola's recommendation (fol. 37) to convert unplayable fingerings to playable ones, even though the resulting pitches may be an octave away from the original ones. Here the musical context suggests **f** as the better note, but this would have to be played as **d**:3, requiring that the **d** be played as **a**:5. The given version, with (open string) **F** instead of **f**, allows the **d** also to be played as an open string (although it can sound only for the value of a dotted minim, since the **d** string is required for the last semiminim **f** in the measure).

46 Here the musical context suggests a semiminim **b̅** ♭, rather than the given **b** ♭. However, with the semibreve **b** ♭ played as **a**:1 and the semibreve **G** as **F**:2, a semiminim **b̅** ♭ (played as **g**:3) might be awkward. The given semiminim **b** ♭ requires only a reiteration of the semibreve note (thus shortening the semibreve in question to a minim).

47 This note is printed as **f** in the H and N copies, while in the A and F copies the lower portion of the letter is missing (it is misinterpreted as **c** in the Eitner edition). Since a minim is explicitly indicated, it is possible that the note an octave lower, **F**, was intended.

48 Here the musical context suggests a minim **f**, rather than the given **F**. The semibreves **a** and **F** cannot be played as open strings because the minim **c** must be fingered as **a**:3, thus requiring the **a** to be played as **F**:4 and the **F** as **C**:5. Following the minim **c**, a minim **f** (**d**:3) would

not be impossible to play, but an **F** (now playable as **F**:0 because the **c** is no longer sounding) would be easier.

49 Here the musical context suggests that this group of four fusas should be an octave higher, although the given reading would be somewhat easier to play.

50 Although the letter indicating the pitch of the third fusa in this group appears to resemble **c**, a close inspection of the shape of the letter reveals it to be a defective **e**, which is the correct pitch (it is interpreted correctly in the Eitner edition, p. 78).

51 Here the two-minim passage **b**♭–**G** would be no more difficult to play an octave higher, which would seem to fit the musical context better.

52 This diagram is essentially the same as the one on the foldout cited on fol. 59 of the 1545 edition (see Appendix 24), the only difference being that the vertical lines of text are replaced by new type (with minor changes) in the latter version. An examination of the two forms of the diagram shows that the quasi-facsimile printed in the Eitner edition between pp. 50 and 51 (p. 5 of these inserted pages) corresponds closely with the 1529 version, while the one printed between pp. 84 and 85 (the appropriate place in Eitner's presentation of the 1529 edition) is in fact the 1545 version.

53 The vertical column at the top centre, obliterated in this facsimile, contains two items (reading from the top): *lā* (referring to the pitch **ā**) and *re*.

54 Although the original refers to courses, reference here is to strings.

55 In the original, several semiminims in the mensural notation have insufficiently inked note-heads, making them seem like minims. Conversely, several minims look like semiminims because their note-heads are clogged.

56 The line under the **G** in the tablature is very faint in the A, F and H copies and missing in the N copy.

57 The last four notes in this bar illustrate Agricola's alternate method of tablature notation for the lower register, consisting of underlined lower-case letters.

58 Similarly, these last four notes are notated in the tablature according to Agricola's alternate method.

59 The four sharped notes in this group are shown in the tablature, while the chromatic inflexions are not explicitly indicated in the mensural notation.

60 Fermatas in the alto and tenor parts are given only in the tablature notation.

61 This pitch is indicated in the tablature as a large lower-case letter. Following Agricola's two methods, it should have been either a capital or an underlined lower-case letter.

62 The 1529 edition gives four lower notes for the bass crumhorn.

63 The 1529 edition gives fingerings for the semitone above the bottom note in all three sizes.

64 The 1529 edition gives a fingering for **G#** in the bass.

65 The 1529 edition gives a fingering for **G#** in the tenor-alto.

66 The 1529 edition gives the fingering ● ○●○ ○○○○ in all three sizes.

67 The 1529 edition does not give this fingering.

68 The 1529 edition gives the fingering ○ ○●● ●●●○ in the treble.

69 The 1529 edition gives the fingering ○ ●●● ●○○○ in the treble.

70 The 1529 edition gives the fingering ○ ●●● ●○○○ in the bass.

71 The 1529 edition gives the fingering ○ ●●● ○○●○ in the bass.

72 The 1529 edition does not give this fingering.

73 The 1529 edition gives the same fingering for this pitch, but both editions are probably in error. (See Appendix 3, note 2.)

74 The 1529 edition gives fingerings for **bb**♭ and **bb**♮ in the tenor-alto.

75 See Appendix 4, note 3.

76 The 1529 edition gives a fingering for these corresponding pitches in the treble and the tenor-alto.

77 The 1529 edition gives only this fingering for the corresponding pitches.

78 The 1529 edition gives two fingerings for these corresponding pitches in the treble and the tenor-alto.

79 Although the bracket that indicates the notes on the treble to which the instruction 'blow moderately' applies reaches only up to this **F**, Agricola probably intended it to be consistent with the corresponding brackets in the tenor-alto and bass fingering charts, in which case it would include also the **G** and the **a**.

80 The 1529 edition gives the fingering ●○● ○●● for the corresponding pitch in the bass.

81 The 1529 edition gives only this fingering for the corresponding pitches.

82 The 1529 edition does not give the corresponding pitches.

83 The 1529 edition gives only this fingering for the corresponding pitches.

84 The 1529 edition gives two fingerings for these corresponding pitches in the treble and the tenor-alto.

85 The 1529 edition gives only this fingering for the corresponding pitches.

86 The 1529 edition also gives the alternate fingering ●●● ○○● for the corresponding pitch in the tenor-alto.

87 The 1529 edition gives fingerings in all three flute sizes for the pitches a whole-tone and a major third above the highest pitch in the present diagram.

88 All of the intervals indicated are tuned exactly according to the Pythagorean system except for the major third (**c̄#**), which approximates the (pure) major third of just intonation. The interval is set by starting at **d̄** and going back the distance of a Pythagorean major ('chromatic') semitone of 5 commas ($\frac{5}{9}$ of a whole-tone, as explained by Agricola on fol. 54 of the 1545 edition).

89 The pitches **g#**, **b̄♭** and **c̄#** are set by starting at the next higher diatonic pitch (**ā**, **b̄♮** and **d̄**, respectively) and going back the distance of a Pythagorean major ('chromatic') semitone of 5 commas. This produces a semitone (**g#**) and a minor third (**b̄♭**) that are very close to their Pythagorean equivalents, and an augmented fourth (**c̄#**) whose tuning approximates that of just intonation. The remaining intervals (whole-tone, major third, fourth, fifth and major sixth) follow the Pythagorean system exactly. Note that the minor sixth (**ē♭**) is not given.

90 This diagram is essentially the same as the one on the foldout cited on fol. 42ᵛ of the 1529 edition. See Appendix 17, note 52.

91 The right-hand vertical column, barely visible in this facsimile, contains letters lined up horizontally with their corresponding numbers and identifying the pitches of the open strings (reading from the bottom to the top) as **Γ**, **C**, **F**, **a**, **d** and **g**.

92 All three citations of **F** in this column are printed without the underline in the original.

93 Tunings that are the same in both methods, or that are given only in method 2, follow the Pythagorean system. Where two tunings are given for each pitch, method 2 follows the Pythagorean system.

94 The proportions presented here, taking into account the corrections, follow the Pythagorean system.

95 This pitch is given inexplicably as **0** in the original.

96 The numerator of this fraction is given incorrectly in the original as 103.

97 This fraction is given incorrectly in the original as $\frac{5}{8}$.

98 Throughout his treatise Agricola uses general terminology for major and minor seconds, thirds, sixths and sevenths, as well as the augmented fourth and diminished fifth, representing the adding together of smaller intervals. The interval from **Γ** to **E**, for example, is expressed as *tonus diapente* ('fifth plus whole-tone'), while *semitonus diapente* indicates the interval a semitone smaller, given here as **Γ** to **D#**. The latter pitch is consistently used as the enharmonic equivalent of **E♭** throughout the treatise.

99 This fraction is given incorrectly in the original as $\frac{16}{81}$.

100 This fraction is given incorrectly in the original as $\frac{8}{81}$.

101 This fraction is given incorrectly in the original as $\frac{1}{3}$.

102 This fraction is given incorrectly in the original as $\frac{1}{3}$.

103 This fraction is given incorrectly in the original as $\frac{23}{81}$.

104 This fraction is given incorrectly in the original as $\frac{3}{32}$.

Index

Many of the terms listed here are found in both singular and plural forms in the text.